'You will never again think of spi[...] story of three children turned i[...] is by turns hilarious, moving and brilliantly told.'
Susan Johnson, author and journalist

'A remarkable glimpse into the shadowy world of Australian espionage and the lasting impact of secrets on a seemingly ordinary family. A story teeming with clandestine assignations, hidden cameras, gangsters, Soviet defectors and informants, all lurking beneath the dreary predictability of suburban life. There are so many double-sided mirrors here that it reads like the very best of spy thrillers.'
Matthew Condon, author of the *Three Crooked Kings* trilogy

'An intimate and compelling look at an ordinary family who happen to be ASIO agents, dressing up, spying on unionists and hiding out with the Petrovs. You will never see suburban Brisbane the same way ever again.'
Kristina Olsson, author of *Boy, Lost* and *Shell*

'A fascinating child's eye-view of the inner and under-life of her ASIO parent-operatives . . . an elusive father, a troubled mother, an afflicted family: A faded world of espionage, lost causes and secretive existences, pretending to normalcy; a world of sexual intrigue and glancing criminality; of Abe Saffron, Charles Spry, Ray Whitrod and the Petrovs.'
Raymond Evans, author of *A History of Queensland*

WITH MY LITTLE EYE

The incredible true story of a family of spies in the suburbs

SANDRA HOGAN

ALLEN&UNWIN
SYDNEY·MELBOURNE·AUCKLAND·LONDON

Allen & Unwin
83 Alexander Street
Crows Nest NSW 2065
Australia
Phone: (61 2) 8425 0100
Email: info@allenandunwin.com
Web: www.allenandunwin.com

A catalogue record for this book is available from the National Library of Australia

ISBN 978 1 76087 846 7

Internal design by Simon Paterson, Bookhouse
Set in 12.6/18.2 pt Bembo MT Pro by Bookhouse, Sydney
Printed and bound in Australia by McPhersons Printing Group

10 9 8 7 6 5 4 3 2

The paper in this book is FSC® certified. FSC® promotes environmentally responsible, socially beneficial and economically viable management of the world's forests.

To Rosa, my mother

It is the absence of facts that frightens people:
the gap you open, into which they pour their fears,
fantasies, desires.

HILARY MANTEL, *WOLF HALL*

CONTENTS

PART 3 THE FAMILY

Prologue

When Sue-Ellen told me about the night it happened, she was nearly sixty. It was the first time she had ever told the story—not just to a journalist, but to anyone. She looked surprised to hear the words coming out of her mouth.

She was seventeen that night in October 1970, and she was out with a boy. They were packed into the sweating, heaving crush at the Davies Park clubhouse in Brisbane, where Johnny O'Keefe was singing, fresh from his tour of Vietnam to rock the Australian troops. The night was hot and the music was pumping. It was exciting, but something was wrong. Sue-Ellen couldn't lose herself in the music, even when Johnny sang 'Shout' and the crowd rose up with a roar and drowned him out.

They left early. She fidgeted, rolling down the window to look out at the casuarinas and blue gums shining in the headlights, then rolling it up again and leaning over to peer at the needle on the speedo. The closer they got to home, the more agitated she became. She didn't know why. It was just one of her feelings. Sue-Ellen knew she wasn't book-smart like her big brother Mark or even her little sister Amanda, but she trusted her feelings.

At the house, someone was watching for her through the screen door—the woman next door. What was she doing there so late? The neighbour pushed open the door and walked out. 'You're home early, Sue-Ellen. Come inside.'

Sue-Ellen wouldn't go in. She was like a spooked horse, refusing to move. 'What happened?' she kept asking. The neighbour had to tell her, right there in the garden.

'Your father has died. I'm so sorry.'

That couldn't be true. Her dad had been getting ready to order chicken and cashews from his favourite Chinese restaurant when she had gone out a few hours before. How could he be dead now?

Sue-Ellen stepped inside this weird house that used to be her comfortable, ordinary home. Her mum and dad should have been sitting quietly in front of the TV, a bottle of XXXX beer on the table, watching one of the endless current affairs programs they loved. Instead, the house was full of people: neighbours, family, friends, members of the Chinese community, police. How did they all get here so quickly? People were passing around plates of Chinese food. She saw her mother in the kitchen, but her mother didn't see her because she was crying and someone was hugging her. Her grandmother sat alone on the sofa in the living room, her head bowed.

There was no sign of her father. She looked for him in every room. Finally, Mark found her. He held her hands. He looked into her eyes. 'Dad had a heart attack,' he said.

'But where is he?' she asked.

'They've taken him to the morgue.'

While she was out of the house on an ordinary date, her dad—her perfectly fine dad—had died. It didn't make sense. She retreated to her bedroom to think it through. Sitting cross-legged on her candlewick bedspread, she thought about how her father often disappeared. There were never any explanations. One day he would be there, the next he'd be gone, for days or weeks—until one day the door would open and he would be there again, safe and sound. Apart from the suitcase in his hand, he would act like it was just a normal day coming home from the office.

Of course, that's what happened, she reasoned. *This is just his biggest disappearing stunt ever.* She would watch out for him and wait, for as long as it took. He would be back.

PART 1

THE CHILDREN

THE CHILDREN

1

Keeping it in the Family

1950s

People always ask why the Dohertys included their children in the secret. Everyone knows that spies have cover stories, even for their children. Sometimes you hear about an adult who discovers on their father's deathbed that he was not really in the import–export business as they had supposed. Or it might have been their mother, whose church and charity work had provided a cover for chatting with strangers. But this news doesn't dramatically change the lives of those grown-up children. They had normal childhoods and the discovery just adds a titillating (or disagreeable) twist to their family story.

These people look sceptical when they hear what the Doherty kids knew and what they did for the Australian Security Intelligence Organisation (ASIO) in the 1950s and '60s. 'How is it even possible to teach little children not to chat about their lives at school?' they ask, shaking their heads. 'What a terrible responsibility for those children.'

Joan and Dudley Doherty fully discussed with each other their decision to be open with the children, even before their first child was born in 1951. It was a matter of principle. Both of them had grown up in families twisted by secrets and lies, and both of them wanted absolute honesty and trust within their family. They would lie for their country—that was their job—but not to their children.

Anyway, it just wasn't practical to keep secrets from the children at first. Both of the older ones, Mark and Sue-Ellen, were born in the middle of 'the case'. Their small living room in Sydney was dominated by a giant listening device trained on the apartment below. It was ASIO's first bugging operation and it caused a lot of commotion in the family home, with agents there day and night listening with massive earphones, transcribing conversations, or translating. Joan was one of those agents wearing earphones, but she also had to keep the children quiet so the work could be done. Even before they could talk, the children knew about work and knew that it was the most important thing. Work came first; the children, much as they were loved, were lower on the list. Espionage was not a day job for the Dohertys—it was their life. It was the air the children breathed.

Principles aside, Dudley simply couldn't resist the opportunity to involve the kids in the work. He was Mr Fix-It, the great problem solver, and he used the materials and the people on hand to do the job. On a farm, he would be the bloke who held machinery or whole buildings together with little bits of wire. As a spy, he made good use of the three kids—Amanda was born later, after they moved to Brisbane—for little jobs. They were willing and teachable, and Dudley could always find something useful for them to do.

From the children's point of view, spying was the only way they could spend time with their dad.

Sometimes Dudley would take one of them with him to work at ASIO's Queen Street office in Brisbane, with strict instructions to be quiet and behave well. They knew it wouldn't be worth the consequences to misbehave at Dad's work. It was usually Sue-Ellen, on the days her mum said she was too noisy and too much trouble. Sue-Ellen didn't care. It was an enormous privilege to spend time with her dad, even if it was just to get her out of her mum's way.

Walking from the car to the office, Sue-Ellen held her dad's hand tightly as they passed through the grounds of the Catholic cathedral. Actually through the grounds! Protestants did not go onto Catholic territory in those days. Sue-Ellen knew they were walking on somebody else's holy land; it felt wicked but exciting. She saw people—they looked just like normal people—hurrying into the cathedral before work. Dad said they were confessing their sins. Protestants didn't need to confess, and Sue-Ellen assumed this was because they were less sinful.

They waited for the green light to cross Elizabeth Street and walked up the GPO laneway to the office, which had a cheery Golden Casket agency in the foyer, selling cigarettes and lottery tickets. The lift door opened and there was Mr Buchanan, the lift driver, with his smiling face. They needed him because there was no numbered floor for the ASIO office and the lift did not stop there automatically. Mr Buchanan could do it, though. He could stop the lift at the secret floor where they got out.

Sue-Ellen was fascinated by Mr Buchanan and she always looked at his feet when they got into the lift. He was an amputee, like her dad, but Mr Buchanan had lost his right leg while her dad had lost his left. Sue-Ellen knew that, if you had an artificial leg, one shoe would always wear out more quickly than the other because, when you were relaxing at home, you would take off the artificial leg. Luckily, her dad and Mr Buchanan had the same shoe size, and they used to buy multiple pairs of sandals and slippers and swap them. Dad would have two left slippers and two left sandals and Mr Buchanan would have two rights of each. At work, they had to wear both shoes so they couldn't share business shoes, but Sue-Ellen still found it interesting to look at their feet in the lift.

When they got out, there was a red-headed lady sitting beside a timber gate. You couldn't get through the barrier unless she pushed a button to let you in. Then there was a long hallway, with cubicles on each side and a dark room off to the right. To get to the offices, you had to go through a huge steel door. Later, she saw a similar one when she watched episodes of *Get Smart*. The Doherty kids knew all about the cone of silence. *Get Smart* made them laugh, as much with relief as anything else, when they recognised their own lives.

Dad would disappear and Sue-Ellen, being very good, would sit quietly with a secretary, who would let her type on the manual typewriter and feed the penny turtles in a tank. Each of the turtles had a name. Sue-Ellen felt a strange mixture of fascination and boredom during the long hours of quiet sitting, wondering what people were doing but knowing she couldn't ask. Bold as she was at home, she could transform herself into a still, quiet person at Daddy's work—a watcher, like him.

Sue-Ellen cherished the drives in the car, which were pretty much the only times she was alone with her dad. Mark got to spend more time with him because a boy made a better cover story for a man. They could be shooting or fishing together, or even just sitting or standing anywhere without attracting attention, especially as Mark was a quiet boy, likely to be thinking about a scientific equation or a rare sea animal while his father was watching something. Amanda, the youngest, was the only one who got real personal time with their dad. She was allowed to sneak into the bedroom on Sunday mornings, while Mum was preparing breakfast, and read the newspaper in bed with him. He read the news and she read the comics. He would tickle her sometimes and call her pet names like Stinker, Lousy Lou Lou and Ratbag.

It's true that agents don't usually tell their husbands or wives—and especially not their children—about their secret work. George Smiley and James Bond are loners because that's how the business works. Security services like it that way because it's a way of protecting national secrets—what your family don't know, they can't tell. And, from a personal point of view, agents feel it keeps their families safer and lets them lead normal lives. But Dudley and Joan Doherty weren't your average ASIO agents. They ran a family operation and they made up their own rules for how to do it. ASIO might have been surprised to find out about it but, in those days, agents operated fairly independently—as long as they strictly carried out the orders they were given.

⌒

Brisbane, May Day 1959

Outside the McWhirters store in the Valley, Dad hoists Sue-Ellen on his shoulders and pushes cheerfully through the crowd to the street front. People are always willing to make room for a child at the front, especially at the Labour Day march.

'There you go, girl,' says Dad, and puts Sue-Ellen down in the gutter to watch the parade. Mum follows in their wake and now stands behind Sue-Ellen, while Dad stops a little distance away with his camera. Mark is eight now and he knows the ropes. He says, 'I'm going to the corner to watch, Dad.'

'Sure, just don't go out of sight.' Dad takes his camera out of its battered leather pouch. It's just an ordinary camera like the other dads have, not one of the ones hidden in books that Sue-Ellen has seen him take to work.

Old men march by in a stately rhythm. Sue-Ellen mainly sees their legs in dark-blue trousers, their black shoes carefully shined. The crowd is quiet enough, though sometimes a child will call out 'Hello, Dad' to one of the men and Sue-Ellen will see him give a quick grin or a wink. Or tip his hat, without changing the expression on his face.

The men all look the same, the way men do when they go to church—properly shaven and cleaned up and a bit solemn. Some of them wear badges on their suit jackets or even ribbons. Sue-Ellen watches out for the big silken banners in bright colours that the men at the front carry. She sees a beautiful one with a big green ship on it.

'What's that one, Daddy?' she calls.

'That's the Waterside Workers. Look at me! Good girl.'

Sue-Ellen hears the camera click. Then Daddy takes a photo of Mark, a bit further up, or that's what it looks like. But Sue-Ellen knows differently. Even if Mark is in the picture, the most important thing is the people behind him and the banner they carry.

In the car, Mum and Dad had said she had to sit or stand where she was told, no questions asked.

'Why?' Sue-Ellen had asked.

'It's Daddy's work,' her mum had replied.

Sue-Ellen had opened her mouth to say 'Why?' again but Mark had kicked her shin quite hard and Sue-Ellen remembered: when it's work, you're not allowed to ask why. She had swallowed her questions and looked out the window at all the suited men and the women in stockings, looking sticky and hot even in May.

She wishes she didn't have to sit still and be quiet for the parade, but Mark has told her they'll go to the exhibition grounds afterwards and there'll be games and sausage rolls and cakes. While the union men are marching, the women are setting up stalls and making everything ready for them.

Sue-Ellen is only six, but she is already good at deferring gratification. She thinks about fairy floss and stays quiet.

⌒

The children assisted in the family business in small ways from the moment they were born. As babes in arms, they helped to provide cover. No one would guess that a young mother with a baby at a cafe table was listening in on a conversation in the next booth, or that a proud dad taking photos of his baby was really interested in the people in the background of the photo.

As soon as each child could walk, Joan would take them out for their daily exercise. A neighbour coming to the window would smile to see the young mother holding her toddler's hand, pointing things out, and bending down to listen with pretty attention to the child's answers. If they could hear the questions she was asking her child, they might have been puzzled. 'Did you see that house we just passed? What colour was the letterbox?' Or 'Did you see someone standing at the window? What did she look like? No, don't look back. They'll see you looking.' Joan was methodically training her chicks in a critical survival skill for agents: awareness of the people and things going on around them.

Whenever there was a march or a parade in town—whether it was for Labour Day or Anzac Day or the Warana spring festival—the Dohertys were part of the crowd. Dudley learned to take photographs so he could collect information on people of interest. Sometimes the children were allowed to take a friend with them; Joan would arrange for the friend to sit a little way away, to provide another angle for the camera. Occasionally Joan would say, 'Ask your dad to take a photo of that float.' Joan didn't say much but the children heard her brief, quiet reports to their dad in the car on the way home. She had noticed everything; her memory was faultless.

Dudley would turn it into a game for the children. He would keep up a run of quiz questions: 'What is that next float going to be? How many people are on the float? Are they men or women? Can you read the name?'

Or he would be looking at the people in the windows along the route. He'd say: 'I have just got to take some photos. Have a look and tell me if there are people on all the balconies. Or if people are sitting down. Or if someone is moving along with the floats. Maybe moving along and then stopping and then following.' He taught them to notice if anything was odd: a man in a group who didn't look like he belonged, or someone whose clothes didn't look right.

They learned spy craft from the time they could listen. If they noticed something a bit different or out of place and mentioned it, they would see their mum and dad give each other a little look and they would feel as if they had got something right.

They knew a lot of things that other kids didn't know. They knew their dad worked for ASIO, and that their mum helped him. They knew it was secret work and that they were helping to defeat communists and keep Australia free. They knew they had to be ready to help at any time, and that work was paramount. They knew that any ordinary-looking person could be someone else and that nothing was quite what it seemed.

But they didn't know some really basic things that their friends at school took for granted. Such as where their dad was when he went away, or what he was doing, or when he would be back. They didn't know who he was watching or who may have been watching them. They didn't know why they did any of the funny things he asked them to do. They knew they would never be answered if they asked, 'Why?' or 'How long?' or 'Who?' or 'Where?' Like child soldiers, they followed orders without question.

Most of the stuff they did know they couldn't tell anyone about. For example, they couldn't talk about the big brown van that used to come to their house to take Dad to work. That was before Amanda was born, when they lived down south. The van had two little portholes at the top and once, thrillingly, Sue-Ellen and Mark were allowed to sit in the van and they could hear their dad talking to someone in another car. At that time even home telephones were uncommon and it seemed like magic. Dad had a dictaphone, too, before they were regularly used in business. When the kids read Dick Tracy cartoons in the paper, they knew the gadgets were real because their dad had the same things, but they couldn't tell anyone.

They couldn't talk about Dad's cameras—a 35 mm Leica in a beautiful leather case and a little Minox the size of a cigarette lighter—or about watching Dad build his own darkroom. He let them see the photos developing and it was magical to watch shapes appear on paper and turn into people's faces. But they couldn't ask who the people were or tell their friends about any of it.

They couldn't talk about Dad's key set or the tin with wax in it that was used for taking key impressions. Or the lock-picking set in a leather roll, like a jewellery roll, only with little pockets. And the triangular tools inside. They got narrower and narrower and narrower. They had points and hooks of all different shapes.

And they certainly couldn't tell anyone the story they loved to hear at home, about the time Dad went to lock-picking classes when he first started working at ASIO. It was a story that Mum told sometimes over dinner. The children's eyes got wide and they looked from Mum to Dad, but he didn't say anything, just listened with the slightest of grins and kept eating. As Mum told it, all the ASIO students had to look out for unpickable locks and practise their skills. Dudley had a great idea for doing this. The following weekend, he broke into Agincourt, the ASIO headquarters in Sydney, and found his way to the office of Director-General Justice Geoffrey Reed. He broke into the office, picked the lock on the director-general's safe and left a note in the safe to say he had been there.

'Were you in big trouble, Dad?' the children asked him.

'ASIO doesn't have lock-picking classes,' said Dad, but he was still grinning.

'Not officially,' said Mum.

The kids knew for a fact that their dad could pick any lock in the world because of the time when Mark and Sue-Ellen had got locked into the subway under the Anzac memorial in Brisbane.

They were living briefly in a boarding house at Upper Edward Street in Brisbane city while they waited for their new house at The Gap to be built. They went off to school on the tram each day and took a shortcut home via the tunnel under Anzac Square. Beside the tunnel's World War I memorial was the Shrine of Memories, a dimly lit and alluring memorial to World War II.

Sue-Ellen and Mark said they were going to go into the shrine to look at something. Amanda said, 'You're going to be in trouble. Mum's going to know.' And Mark said, 'Only if you tell her.' So Amanda went home and didn't tell.

But then she had to tell, because the others didn't come home. When Mark and Sue-Ellen decided to leave the shrine, as the sun was going down, they found themselves locked in behind heavy iron bars. They shook the bars, called out and tried every exit—but there was no way out. After an hour or two, their absence was noted at home. Joan began to worry and Amanda confessed.

Dudley rang the council and they went, 'Hmmmm. Hmmmm.' They talked about call-out fees and forms to be filled in. They were going to charge to send someone out. Dudley told them not to worry. He walked down to the shrine and found Mark and Sue-Ellen clinging to the bars and watching out anxiously.

'Go to the back of the shrine and try the other gate,' he said.

'We've done it a hundred times,' said Sue-Ellen. 'It won't open.'

'Just try it one more time,' said Dad.

Mark and Sue-Ellen went to check the other gate again and gave it one more hopeful push. It didn't budge. They ran back to the front gate and found it was now mysteriously open. They knew not to ask any questions. They hadn't even seen Dad holding the lock-picking kit, but he must have had it. Dad didn't like them to watch him doing stuff like that. They ran home to dinner and a big talking-to from Mum.

Sometimes knowing but not telling was complicated. For example, if Uncle Mick, one of their ASIO uncles, came over for tea, the kids might sit on his lap and hug him. But if they were outside the house and they saw him anywhere, they knew that they were not to say hello to him or even to flick their eyes towards him. Uncle Mick might be working.

They knew that other kids didn't do what they did, but it still seemed normal for them. It didn't feel like they were doing anything out of the ordinary. Nothing seemed strange to them at the time. And they trusted their parents to keep them safe. As long as they followed the rules.

2

Learning to be Invisible

By the time the kids could actively help with ASIO work, they were living at the house at The Gap. In those days, working-class Brisbanites lived in timber houses in the inner-city suburbs and the new professional classes had double-brick houses built further out in leafy suburbs like The Gap. Their house wasn't so fancy that it stood out, but it was nice. It had a double garage and a big garden. Joan liked to mention that their neighbours included an obstetrician, an opera singer and the head of cruise line P&O; the kids laughed about their mum being a snob. A police commissioner (not yet known to be corrupt) lived nearby, as did a prominent newspaper editor and a Wallabies rugby player.

The Dohertys moved into their new house on Kilmaine Street on 22 November 1963, a date they never forgot because it was the day that JFK was assassinated in Dallas. The shooting death of an American president meant that secret agents all over the world had their leave cancelled—even Dudley Doherty, far away in Brisbane, Australia. Dudley went to work to follow the assassination news on a crackly black-and-white television and make plans to defend democracy. Joan had to move house on her own, with dubious help from three excited children aged between five and twelve.

It was heavy work to carry their few bits of furniture and boxes of clothes into the house because of the steep front yard, a common feature in their hilly suburb. Once inside, the children ran through the house, looking eagerly out the back windows to a rough paddock. Nobody knew who owned the paddock, but they soon found that all the neighbourhood children played there. The Dohertys' block had been part of a farm not too long before. When Joan walked around the yard with the children, she found marijuana growing. She recognised it immediately—it was part of her training—and quietly instructed the children to pull it out.

Joan grew a garden from cuttings. She carried scissors in her bag wherever she went and discreetly clipped any interesting new plants she saw. The garden was rocky because the neighbourhood was built on a granite outcrop, so Joan organised the children to fill buckets with rocks to be used for rock gardens or pathways.

As soon as they had settled in, Amanda began attending the local government primary school in The Gap while Sue-Ellen and Mark continued at their school at Ashgrove. Amanda had a friend called Tracey whom she envied, because her father was a milkman. When she visited Tracey on weekends, they were allowed to wash the milk van and, if they found any loose change when they were cleaning, they could keep it. Amanda wanted to have a dad with an exciting job like that.

In those days, it was usual for teachers to go around the classroom asking each child what their father did. (Mothers were assumed not to be working.) The Doherty kids were prepared for this question in the way that all ASIO children were prepared: they answered that their father worked in the public service. The idea was to make it sound quite boring so that nobody would ask any more questions. Other kids had fathers whose jobs had exciting perks—like one who worked at the markets and brought home leftover fruit—and there would be lots of questions for them, but no one ever raised their hand to ask the Doherty kids about their dad's job.

Sometimes a teacher would not accept the standard 'public service' answer and would ask one of the children which department their father worked in. If that occurred, Joan had instructed them to say that he worked in the Attorney-General's Department. That piece of information was guaranteed to kill any conversation stone dead. It was an example of the principle Joan taught her children: to always tell the truth but to not tell everything.

'Attorney-General's Department' was such a nondescript term that Amanda had difficulty remembering it. She practised it in her head on the way to school. *Attorney-General's Department. Attorney-General's Department.* And then she forgot anyway and had to go home and ask. Joan would say 'Amanda!' quite crossly. Amanda finally memorised it and never forgot it again.

Mark just accepted the rule. He knew his dad didn't do a normal job, but it was just something they didn't discuss outside the family. Sue-Ellen would never say what her father really did but she felt free to make up other jobs for him. No way was she going to give that boring line about the attorney-general. Most often she would say he was a policeman and he had a gun. It wasn't exactly a lie because her dad was a member of the police rifle club. Mark had told her about it because Dudley sometimes took him rabbit shooting or target shooting, and he said their dad was a pretty good shot. They used the old .303 rifles that had been used in the war—single bolt action, single shot. Mark said they often had to stop and wait for kangaroos to bounce away before they could start firing again because it wasn't good form to shoot kangaroos.

Amanda didn't like guns, but she was proud of her job of cleaning the ammunition for her dad and the policemen with their motorbikes and leather jackets. She had a special cloth and she cleaned all the bullets and counted them. She put the ammunition carefully into boxes. She cut up bits of cloth for the men to use to clean the barrels of the guns. She grew up loving the smell of camphor.

One of the first jobs the children did to help Dudley was surveillance. 'Come on kids, we're going out in the car,' he would say. They knew exactly what that meant: get up straightaway; fetch some toys, a jumper and a change of clothes; and assemble in the neutral-coloured Holden that ASIO had adapted for Dudley to drive with his wooden leg.

He would drive several times around a really big block. As they passed one particular building—sometimes it was

Brisbane's Trades Hall, sometimes a private house—the three children might be sitting in the front seat of the car. (This was in the days before seatbelts.) The next time they passed it, two children would be in the back seat and one hiding on the floor. They kept changing clothes and popping up and down, so they were never in the same configuration.

Dressing up and making quick costume changes were important skills for the children as soon as they could do up their own buttons and tie their laces. The point was not to look attractive or to draw attention, but the opposite—to look so average they were invisible. They were right there but no one noticed them.

They didn't know why they were doing it, just that they were helping Daddy with his work. They knew they couldn't argue or delay. They did what he instructed them to do and felt proud to help him. He was playing a funny game with them. It made them feel important and usually it was fun.

3

I Spy with My Little Eye

In the fifties and sixties, Brisbane families entertained themselves with Sunday drives. They piled into the cars the fathers had polished and drove around just for the pleasure of it. There were no motorways or toll points or traffic jams, and it didn't take long to get out of the city and into the countryside. You drove through suburbs where every second house had a chook run and every street had a corner store that supplied the things that weren't delivered by the milko, the ice man, the bread van or the fisho. A little bit further and you were driving on dirt roads where little stalls with honesty boxes offered fresh pineapples or mangoes or honey. You didn't need a GPS then and people talked or sang in the car, or just looked out the windows.

The Dohertys were enthusiastic Sunday drivers but they never gazed idly out the window. Dudley always had something for the kids to do. A routine activity was the numberplate run. They would drive to a building and each child would check a numberplate. As they drove past, they would call out which colour car they were picking. 'I'll take the white car,' Sue-Ellen might say. 'I'll have the grey,' Mark would say. Amanda would pick one too, and their dad would take the rest. After they drove past, the children would describe the car, call out the numberplate of the car, and say where it was parked and whether it was the first or last car in the driveway. Sometimes they would do a second run, hours later, to see which cars were still there.

Or they might drive an hour and a half north to Dicky Beach on the Sunshine Coast. Other kids went swimming and built sandcastles if they went to the beach, but not the Dohertys. Dad would say they were going to visit his old friends Roy and Pearl, but the kids knew the main point of the exercise was checking numberplates outside a house on the next block, where one of the communist leaders lived.

It was a serious task. The kids knew they couldn't make anything up. If they were sent out to remember a numberplate and they didn't remember a letter, they couldn't come back and say that they thought it was this number or this letter. There was no 'maybe'. There was no 'it could have been'. They were trained in precise observation.

Dad didn't play cricket or help with their homework, but he took them to Speakers' Corner. It was at Centenary Place, a pretty wedge of grass in Fortitude Valley, dominated by a statue of Robbie Burns, the Scottish poet of the people. Centenary Place was designated as the people's forum in 1962, the year Australia entered the Vietnam War. Even before conscription started, anti-war protesters stood on soapboxes, roaring at the crowd, calling Prime Minister Menzies a filthy warmonger. Lots of people came to watch because it was one of the most fun places to be on a Sunday afternoon in Brisbane then. And it was educational.

The children watched Aboriginal activists at Centenary Place and were almost the only children at their school who knew that their country had been owned by Aboriginal and Torres Strait Islander people for at least 40,000 years before Captain Cook arrived. Other speakers waved their Bibles and showered spit on upturned faces as they described the glories of the Second Coming. The children were most interested in the speakers who told how they had met aliens from other planets or even been on their spaceships. Dad would have to drag them away from the UFO people if he wanted to take their photos in front of one of the other speakers. He took photos of the speakers who got the biggest crowds, whatever they were talking about.

When the ASIO uncles came to visit the Dohertys at home, the kids heard the names these men gave to the people they watched: they called them 'politicals', 'ferals' or 'crackpots'. The official ASIO name for them was 'speakers of influence'. ASIO was interested in anyone in the public eye, whatever their interests, because you never knew what they might be a front for, or who might be using them. Dudley didn't call people names, though. The way the kids saw it, he was just interested in people; he wanted to know what made them tick.

Sometimes one of the children was with their dad when he had a friendly chat with a belly dancer in a small house in Coorparoo. At a time when women's make-up was generally modest, the children were fascinated by her full red lips and the way she painted her eyes to look like a big cat's. Dad would offer her a cigarette and lean his head forward to light it for her as they sat in her little kitchen with its beaded curtains. His eyes would twinkle at her while they chatted about people she knew in a lazy, friendly way. Sometimes she would offer the children scented Turkish delight from a big gold box.

A regular place they went with Joan and Dudley was the Trades Hall building on Turbot Street. It was union headquarters, home to the Trades & Labor Council of Queensland, and the bustling venue for meetings, social events, and training and education for the state's highly unionised workforce. Trades Hall has long been demolished, replaced in the eighties by the high-rise, glass-fronted IBM building, but in those days it was a grand building, if a little shabby—an important centre in Brisbane.

The whole family would drive around the building two or three times to see if there was any movement. Then Dudley would park the car and stroll towards the building. The children knew he had some small concealed equipment on him: his mini-camera and dictaphone. He might have had other gadgets they didn't know about—they always wondered what he put inside his wooden leg. Then he would sit on a bench with a newspaper and watch who walked in and out and what cars were there. Mum and the kids wandered around in King Edward Park, with its green benches and shady terraces, and Mark and Sue-Ellen raced each other up Jacob's Ladder, the huge, impossibly steep staircase up to Wickham Terrace.

Their mum tried to make Sunday drives fun for the children. They visited an informant at Samford, north-west of the city, who had a poddy calf and, if the children put their hands inside the calf's mouth, it would suck their fingers. Their mum would take the children around the farm collecting manure in a sack to take home for their garden.

She organised games for road trips, like Spotto. The kids would have to yell out 'Spotto!' if they saw a yellow car, or anything else she named, and the first one to call 'Spotto!' was the winner. Joan kept score with precision and absolute fairness and the winner got a serve of the large supply of apples and oranges she had cut up before they left home. Naturally, they also played I Spy.

'I spy with my little eye . . . a dark shape behind that curtain.'

Joan always packed a picnic lunch in a basket and, at lunchtime, she would lay out a cloth in a field or a park, hand out sandwiches and pour hot tea from a tartan thermos flask.

A special treat for the children was going to the port to visit big ships when they came into Brisbane. If Brisbane was the first port of call for a cargo ship coming from Europe or Asia, Dudley and his partner Mick would go to the port to check out the people on the ship. The pair wore plain clothes but they walked on board with the customs officers in their smart uniforms and nobody ever asked them who they were. People naturally assumed they had some authority.

Dudley and Mick walked around the ships, chatting to people and looking around. Being the engaging bloke that he was, Dudley often found himself invited to dinner on a ship, and he would bring the family. Including his family was always a great way to relax the people he sought information from, and to get them chatting.

The children sat at the captain's table for dinner. Once they were on an American ship at Thanksgiving and they ate turkey and cranberry sauce. The idea of having meat with jam on it was thrilling and bizarre and the children all eagerly accepted second helpings, after glancing at Mum to see if it was okay. They ate their dinner quickly and, while Mum and Dad stayed talking, the children ran through the ship, playing hide and seek. The staff on board were funny and kind and they encouraged the children to run and whoop and giggle. It was a rare opportunity for the Doherty kids to run free.

Normally they were not allowed to run amok like they did on the ships—even in their own home, because their dad might be tired, or reading the paper. And Dudley, who worked all the time, would have to be exhausted to the point of illness before he would consider taking a holiday. The Dohertys only ever went on holidays twice and the children never forgot those times. The first time, they went to the Gold Coast. The kids were so excited they couldn't sleep for days before they left. At last the day arrived for them to pile into the car and drive south. When they arrived at the Santa Fe motel with its lino floors and bunk beds, the children peeled themselves off the hot seats of the Holden and demanded to go to the beach.

'Shhhh,' said Joan. 'Your dad's exhausted.' Dudley went straight to sleep, with Joan fiercely guarding his rest while she made salads for lunch. The children tiptoed out of the house to explore on their own. They were allowed to swim in the swimming pool where Joan could watch them from the hotel window, but not to go to the beach. The next morning, their dad woke at 4 a.m. and went fishing. He was home and asleep again, with fish on the bench for Joan to cook, by the time the children got up, so they still couldn't go to the beach. That turned out to be the pattern of their days.

Near the end of their holiday week, Dudley had recovered enough to go to the beach with his family. As the children gambolled and hopped across the hot sand, he and Joan stepped slowly, finding a place among the sunbathers where they could lay their towels. 'Come in, Dad, come in,' yelled Sue-Ellen.

'Coming ready or not!' he yelled back, grinning. Still standing, he took off his shirt and tie and folded them neatly on the sand. He unbuckled his belt and let his trousers drop to the sand, revealing his Speedos. He folded the trousers too and laid his hat on top. Finally he sat down, removed one shoe and sock, then carefully unstrapped his wooden leg with its flexible rubber foot, sliding off the woollen sock over the stump beneath. He laid these items carefully beside the little pile of his things. Then gazing steadily at the surf, he hopped down to the water and stood on one leg until the water lifted him up, allowing him to sit in the shallows. There he sat in the bliss of sun and water, splashing himself and cheerfully calling out instructions to Mark and Sue-Ellen on catching waves. Amanda was too little to go in. When he'd had enough, he hopped back up the beach towards his leg. They always had to find a place to sit on the tideline, where the hard sand began, because Dudley couldn't hop on the soft sand.

At the age of fifteen, Dudley had swung cheekily off the wrong side of a Sydney tram. He fell as he tried to dodge an oncoming car, and the steel blade of the tram neatly sliced off his leg. He survived and even sat his matriculation exam ten days later. He always told the kids that surviving the accident had taught him that nothing was impossible. Nothing and no one can stop you from doing the things you really want to do, he told them. He never asked for help and nobody ever felt sorry for him.

Those golden sun-and-sand days were rare enough to be remembered for a lifetime. The second time they went on holidays, they drove to Cotton Tree Beach on the Sunshine Coast. Mark got an ear infection and also cut his foot on barnacles on the very first day. After that he wasn't allowed to swim for the whole holiday. Amanda had broken her arm falling off a fence, just before they came, so she missed out too. On the final day of the holiday, a cyclone blew up and they all stayed inside drawing Rocky and Bullwinkle cartoons by candlelight.

These were the days before people had 'lifestyles' but, even so, the Dohertys weren't good at leisure. They were a working family.

4

Secrets in a Box

Amanda wakes one morning in her little single bed at The Gap and sees an exquisite dark-haired girl fast asleep in the spare bed next to hers. She stares, not sure if she is still asleep and dreaming. The girl is so beautiful— surely she can't be real. Amanda looks around the room to check if she is really awake. A magnificent gold-trimmed kimono is hanging on the wardrobe door, with tiny silk shoes on the floor below it. Elaborate hair jewels, with cherry blossom flowers and glittering gems, are on the dresser.

There is a Japanese geisha girl in Amanda's bedroom.

Amanda jumps out of bed and dresses quietly in her school clothes so as not to disturb her visitor. She runs to the kitchen where her mother is preparing breakfast. Her mother gives her the look, meaning 'We don't talk about this', so Amanda just eats her breakfast without asking any questions. She plaits her hair, gets into the car and goes to school, not saying a word to anyone, even her best friend Tracey. That afternoon she runs home from school, but the geisha girl and all her belongings are gone.

After that, Amanda is never quite sure that it really happened.

It wasn't until she was grown up, with a child of her own, that Amanda felt safe to mention the geisha girl to Sue-Ellen. Could it have been a dream? What a relief it was—having grown up in a world where nothing was certain and you could only rely on your own senses—to discover that Sue-Ellen had seen her too. The geisha girl was one of the people Dad had brought back from the ships when he went down to inspect them for ASIO. Sue-Ellen had been home from school that day with strep throat and she saw her dad leaving the house with the girl to take her back to the ship. Sue-Ellen was watching from her bedroom window, standing back a little so no one could see her (instinctively adopting the classic position for watchers) and she saw the girl was crying as she got into the car.

Visitors were part of Dad's work, which meant no one was allowed to ask questions—however strange or interesting or spooky the person might be. Another time, little Amanda woke up and found a strange man in the spare bed in her bedroom. She saw an unfamiliar uniform draped over a hanger. 'Good morning,' she said, and no more. She knew the rules. Visitors were people Dad worked with or whom he met at work; they could be colleagues or informants or even targets, so you were polite but you didn't chat.

You didn't chat but no one stopped the children from watching carefully and drawing their own conclusions. Although they always had to follow the visitors-are-Daddy's-work rule, the kids were pretty sure the geisha girl was just one of Dad's 'cases'. Dad's cases were usually people he met at work whom he took in out of kindness. They may not have been actually part of his work. He did it because of the Salvos. As a one-legged boy, with no visible father, Dudley had received a lot of help from the Salvation Army. They had helped him get an education and a job, and he'd had fun and made friends playing the euphonium in the Salvation Army band. He said he owed it to the Salvos to be kind to people.

If he saw a story in the paper about a kid who had been in an accident and had an amputated limb, he would find out what hospital they were in, drop everything and head down to visit them. Sometimes he took the children with him. They would sit quietly while he chatted to the injured kid. He didn't just talk either. He had a way of getting the kid to talk about their fears and sadness and he listened in the way he had that always made people feel special. Then he would pull up his trouser leg to reveal his wooden leg. Once they'd taken it in, he would explain how good his life was—great job, beautiful wife, kids, the lot. 'You can do anything you want,' he would say, and he meant it.

The Doherty children didn't always think it was a good idea for Dad to be so kind to people. He gave away anything in the house to people in need, including the children's brand-new Christmas presents. The children felt anxious whenever they heard anyone tell a hard-luck story because they knew they were likely to lose something they cared about. They especially hated it if someone told him their pet had died, because Dad would immediately give them his own family's dog or cat. The Dohertys never owned an animal for its whole life. Pets were always given away.

Joan always had food in the freezer for extra people. As well as waifs and strays, there were the ASIO uncles, who might come at any time of the day or night, and the new recruits. They all loved Joan's excellent cooking. Dudley kept her supplied with food, even when money was short. Sometimes he brought home half a sheep—from who knows where. Like Robin Hood, Dudley would redistribute much of the booty to other people. Once when his friend Uncle Roy was unemployed, Aunty Pearl opened her fridge after Dudley had visited and found a whole smoked salmon in it. She had never seen a whole smoked salmon in her life.

Occasionally, one of the visitors became their friend. Black Americans had been banned from performing in Australia in 1928 and, even in the sixties, Mark had to import LPs of his favourite black American blues singers. The only black American singers played on Brisbane radio were white-sounding singers like Nat King Cole. In these racially restricted times, the Dohertys periodically entertained a mysterious visitor from the ships called Arthur Goldstein, who was not only black but Jewish. He was kind and funny and handsome. Both the girls were in love with Arthur and his shiny uniform with brass buttons. Mark remembered Arthur fondly because he brought whole boxes of Milky Ways and other treats that weren't available in Australia at the time. They didn't know who Arthur Goldstein was, or what he was doing in their living room, but he was a shining light of their childhood.

Dudley's general approach to his informants was to make them his friends. It is unlikely that he had a budget to pay people for information. He just got to know them, and they got to like him and feel free to talk to him. He was always willing to lend people a hand. With the Chinese community, this took the form of helping them negotiate immigration regulations and bring their relatives out to work in their restaurants. The Doherty kids remembered him helping restaurateur Johnny Go bring his mail-order bride into the country before there was an industry to do that. He sat beside Johnny encouragingly while he filled in the forms, answering questions when needed, and he found out where to send the completed paperwork. He may have had a quiet word in the right ear as well, to make sure there were no unnecessary obstacles. Another time he helped a Chinese family who couldn't have children to adopt one of their sister's children. The sister in China had many children and was happy that one of them could have a good life in Australia.

The Chinese community treated Dudley like a god because of all the help he gave them, and his children were part of their lives. The Dohertys were often guests at Chinese parties and dinners. Amanda and Sue-Ellen wore cheongsams and used chopsticks with ease; Sue-Ellen wore her blonde hair in Chinese pigtails. They knew a few Chinese greetings and they could understand more of what was said in Chinese than they let on. Sometimes they stayed for a weekend with Chinese friends. They never paid for Chinese food anywhere they went—any attempts to pay were treated as an insult. Most of their friends were Chinese in those days, and they were the only non-Chinese at the parties.

The Chinese children were curious about Dudley and he used to let them climb all over him. One day the Dohertys were visiting a Chinese family and one of the children sat under the table and put tokens from a boardgame into the ventilation holes of Dad's wooden leg. He had to withdraw to the bathroom for some time to clear out his leg before they could leave.

Chinese people were their best friends, but friendship wasn't straightforward. The children were taught to be careful of everyone, even their friends. Dudley used to tell them, 'When it comes down to it, the Chinese trust the Chinese. They don't trust us.'

Later, that made sense to the kids. Why should Chinese people trust the man who was paid to spy on them? Not that he would have told them he was spying, but they must have wondered why this bloke from the government was always around asking questions. There was give and take between them, affection and much kindness, but it was not a situation that would permit intimacy and trust.

Like most ASIO officers, Dudley didn't speak Chinese, but he found he had a skill for communicating without words. Once Sue-Ellen was with him when he walked into the kitchen of a Chinese restaurant. Although her dad didn't speak Chinese and the staff didn't speak English, she saw them communicate easily using gestures and smiles. Fascinated, she asked him how he did it.

'People are always telling you what they want and need,' he said. 'You simply have to match them. If they're quiet, you're quiet.'

In January 1967, the Dohertys heard on the news that a bomb had exploded at the office of the Yugoslav Consulate-General in Sydney's Double Bay. Suddenly Dudley was taking his family with him to noisy backyard dinners at long tables in the homes of people whose names always seemed to end in 'titch', or so the kids thought. Mysteriously, these people were not communists—in fact they were the opposite—but ASIO still had to watch them.

So the children had to remember that when they went to 'Aunty Helen's' place they were not to mention the names of any other Yugoslav families, or anything they had eaten in their houses, or anything they heard there. The children didn't know at the time which families were Serbian and which were Croatian or Macedonian and they didn't know that some of them were terrorists—they just knew that you didn't talk about any of the Titches to each other. And you didn't tell them anything about yourself either.

It was hard, especially for little Amanda. When she met anyone, she had to think, *Who are you? Who else do you know? Who else am I allowed to talk about that you might know? Who am I not allowed to talk about? What can I say? What am I supposed to do?*

Sue-Ellen learned to just say nothing, because she was never sure of the right thing to say. If anyone asked her opinion or even what she had been doing, it felt like a challenge. She would withdraw into silence for fear of saying the wrong thing.

When Sue-Ellen wasn't sure if she was allowed to know about something she had seen or heard, she had a technique she thought of as 'putting it in a box'. She pictured part of her mind as a very strong safe with a combination lock. She visualised herself putting each fact into the safe and locking it.

She never discussed this with anyone but, when she grew up, she found out that Amanda had also pictured herself putting secrets into a box when she was a child.

They all knew that if someone wanted to be their friend, they should be cautious, even suspicious. Why did this person want to be their friend? The person might have motives that were dangerous to their family—or to the world. The danger was never spelled out, but the children all felt it. They all had little nervous habits. Sue-Ellen had frequent dreams of running away: some invisible, terrifying, enormous something was pursuing her.

Mum and Dad tried to keep things clear for the children. They gave them a list of people they could trust. It was a very small list: Dad's mother, Grandma Doris, and her husband, Grandpa Jack; ASIO 'uncles' Mick and Bill; and Aunty Pearl and Uncle Roy. Even with people on the list, you didn't talk openly unless it was an emergency. Need-to-know still operated with close family members. If Sue-Ellen asked whether she could talk about their lives to anyone else, a school friend or a kind neighbour, Joan would simply ask, 'Are they on the list?'. The children understood that there were people on the list, and that everyone else was Dad's work.

Another thing they had to do to keep safe was to pay attention to what clothes they wore. Dudley didn't wear fake moustaches or wigs, but he could camouflage himself to fit in anywhere and talk to anyone about anything. The children also learned to dress up to fit into any environment. You wore different clothes for visiting Chinese or Yugoslavs and, for Anglo-Australians, you blended in by wearing the most ordinary of outfits for that occasion.

Wherever they were, they had to be careful not to say the wrong thing. They were not even sure if they could talk about what Dad did at work in front of Grandma Doris.

They yearned to stand out—not to be average and invisible. They begged Dad to get a different kind of car, not the Holden that no one noticed. 'What about a Falcon, Dad?' begged Amanda.

'Nup,' he said.

'Or at least get a Holden that's a really good colour.'

'Nup.'

When it was Dad's birthday, the kids went shopping together for a tie. They spent ages considering fat ties and striped ties and ties with naked ladies on them. But it was no use. In the end, they had to sadly admit he wouldn't wear anything but the standard blue office tie he always wore.

When Grandma Doris made their clothes, they always begged her for some feature that made the clothes stand out a little, even if it was just a different colour for the collar or an unusual button. Mark carefully customised the slot cars he played with under the house. He might look like an average kid, but he decided that his slot cars would be unique—different from all the other boys'.

Every six weeks, Dudley would go to Central and North Queensland for work. He didn't say what work was involved, but Mark knew he was checking on the Chinese people. When he was nine or ten, Mark sometimes went away with his dad. Mostly Dudley would leave him to read a book while he went and chatted to somebody but, in Rockhampton, Mark played chess with an old Chinese man while they both waited for Dad to return from interviewing people at the waterfront and in the Chinese restaurants. Unlike Sue-Ellen, who was noisy and endlessly curious, Mark fitted perfectly into the family trade. He followed instructions precisely, content to sit and read wherever he was left. He liked reading anything from comics to science books, and was fascinated by chemistry and outer space and deep sea creatures. His father's activities, by contrast, appeared supremely uninteresting, so Mark was happy to take whatever perks came along and forget whatever he heard, as required.

The kids didn't mention to their friends at school that they ate Chinese food. That wasn't a secret, but they couldn't have talked about it without drawing attention to themselves. In those days, there were fewer restaurants in Brisbane and many people didn't go out for dinner. For their school friends, Chinese food would have seemed so foreign and exotic as to be downright suspicious. Nor did they mention their friendships with people in the Chinese community. Why would you have Chinese friends? At school they needed to be like everyone else, and that would have marked them out as seriously weird. For the kids at school, 'normal' people were white and either Catholic or Anglican, maybe Methodist. At lunchtime they ate Vegemite sandwiches, made from shop-bought white bread. The Greek and Italian immigrant kids were considered 'foreign', as were pizza and pasta. So, like chameleons, the Doherty children adapted, conforming to the average in whatever world they found themselves in.

Australian culture in the fifties and sixties was drab, white and conformist. International travel was expensive and rare. The fact that the children were exposed to different cultures, languages and foods was a privilege and one they knew to keep to themselves. Not drawing attention to yourself was a spy thing, but it was also an important survival skill in the narrow enclave of British descendants perched on the eastern coast of this ancient land, where not even the original inhabitants were acknowledged and only Anglo newcomers were welcome.

5

Rules

Being an ASIO family meant there were rules for everything. Dudley was the boss of the house and Joan was his second-in-command. Their dad was usually out working, so the children obeyed their mum without question. They knew that if she gave a certain look or a particular turn of the head, they must not cross her. She did not raise her voice, but there were rules for every situation. The most important rules were about what you could tell or not tell people, but related to that were rules about honesty. *Never lie but keep the whole truth for inside the family.* Because the rules of telling and not telling had been in place as soon as they could speak, none of children can remember how and when they were first told.

But in the military-style organisation of Doherty family life, many additional subsidiary rules had to be remembered and followed to the letter. As well as the usual kinds of rules about table manners and punctuality, there were rules about how to look and behave in every situation. Making a noise was almost always prohibited. 'Where is Dad?' was a forbidden question. So were 'What is he doing?' and 'Why can't I go too?'

There were rules about when they could talk to their dad. When he came home from work, they weren't allowed to talk to him at all for the first half-hour. Mum said he needed to rest. He'd either go into their bedroom or he'd change his clothes and go outside and water the garden. And at night he would listen to the news and finish reading the papers with Mum and they were not allowed to talk then either. The children were never allowed to criticise their dad, or to ask questions or interrupt him.

As the girls grew up, there were rules about who they could go out with, and unbreakable curfews. Dudley also instructed them on who they could *not* marry: motorcycle cops and Yugoslavians were out. No questions asked.

The children understood rules were for safety—their own, maybe other people's, maybe even the nation's. They tried to follow the rules and accepted their punishments if they didn't. Amanda struggled conscientiously but found it difficult and worrying. Mark did what he was told but found ways to be individualistic; at high school, he wore his hair long and later, shockingly, he took up left-wing politics. Generally, Amanda and Mark found it easy to comply because they could do the things they liked best without breaking any rules: they both enjoyed sitting quietly and reading. Sue-Ellen didn't. She found out about the world by poking it with sticks and asking questions. Sue-Ellen was what was known then as a street angel and a home devil. She complied with all the rules in public, but at home she tested her parents to the limit.

When Sue-Ellen was little, she thought her mother was too busy with the baby to talk to her. Mark was always reading a book. Daddy was always working. Sue-Ellen made sure they knew she was there, though. She complained loudly and continuously; she didn't put her clothes away; she didn't take the rubbish out. When her mother put the hot iron out on the stairs to cool and told Sue-Ellen to be very careful of it, Sue-Ellen said yes and then ran down the stairs and bumped the iron. The hot, flat part of the iron fell on her back. 'You naughty girl! I told you,' said Joan, looking at the scorch mark on Sue-Ellen's back. Sue-Ellen, crying with pain, couldn't see her mother's frightened face; she only heard the angry voice.

'Wait till your father gets home,' her mum would say. When Dad did come home from work, Joan would say, 'Wait till you hear what she did today.' And she'd tell him the latest story of Sue-Ellen's defiance. Dad would change instantly from being calm to being furious and he'd reach for the belt. He didn't give Sue-Ellen a chance to speak; he just gave her a hiding.

One day, Dad said to seven-year-old Sue-Ellen, 'Right. You're getting a belting.'

And Sue-Ellen said, 'You've got to catch me first,' knowing that she could run faster than he could with his wooden leg. She ran down the stairs and he thumped down them after her. Looking back, she saw her dad's face was an angry mask; he was determined to catch her and thrash her. She screamed with fear and excitement. She ran to shelter behind the orange tree. Dad feinted and she ran one way only to find him towering over her. He grabbed her with one hand and thrashed her with the other. Later, Mum said that he had damaged his wooden leg when he chased her and it had cost him £70 to get a new leg—that was two months' worth of wages. *Good!* thought Sue-Ellen, but she didn't dare say it out loud.

⌒

If Sue-Ellen got through a week without a belting, she would look back and think, *What was different about that week?* Grandma Doris used to say to Sue-Ellen, 'Girl, you upset the equilibrium.' Sue-Ellen had no idea what she meant. Her own opinion was that she had been adopted. Sue-Ellen got to talk about it with Grandma Doris because, after a while, that's who Dad took her to every Saturday morning, and left her for the weekend. It was with Grandma Doris and her step-grandfather Grandpa Jack that Sue-Ellen lived her other life—a life in which she felt safe and free, without a lot of rules.

Doris and Jack's house in Milton, one of Brisbane's inner riverside suburbs, was a tiny wooden cottage, set above the road. The dark kitchen was so small it only fitted a table and three, maybe four chairs, but you couldn't push the chairs back because they would hit the wall. Next to the kitchen was a sewing room where Doris kept her machine set up permanently. First there was an old pedal-operated Singer and later an electric Pfaff machine, set in a proper timber sewing table with drawers. There were huge jars of buttons that Sue-Ellen played with. She used the large ones to make yo-yos and, when Grandma Doris wasn't looking, played with the big pinking shears, cutting scraps of cloth into strips.

Grandma Doris was a gifted dressmaker and she was always making sailor dresses and gingham smocks for Sue-Ellen to wear with sandals, or with white bobby socks and court shoes for going out. Whenever Sue-Ellen stood still long enough, her grandma would have her standing on the table to check a hem or pin up a new dress. And then she'd slap her on the bottom and send her off to run around in the garden. Grandma Doris was a snappy dresser herself, and she stood out from the crowd with her statuesque figure encased in bodiced dresses in black, brown, burnt orange and grey. She worked in a shoe store and always had good shoes. She encouraged Sue-Ellen's lifelong love of beautiful, well-made shoes.

Doris was a big, comfortable woman, always ready with a cuddle for Sue-Ellen, and Grandpa Jack was a good huggable size as well. He always wore a felt hat with a big brim tilted at a jaunty angle and a collared shirt, and he carried a Gladstone bag. He took that bag with him to the race meetings on Sundays, and every Saturday afternoon he listened to the races on the wireless set in the kitchen.

Grandpa Jack was a gambler and he knew the heritage of every horse on the track. A young boy across the road used to come over to visit Jack for special coaching. The boy wanted to be a race caller when he grew up because he was mad keen on horses. They would occupy the kitchen table and Jack would listen intently while the boy called races they had both listened to previously on the radio. Jack would put on his own special calling voice to demonstrate the right way to do it, if the boy slipped up.

It was thanks to Grandpa Jack's gambling that he and Doris had a television at their house, long before anyone else had one, even though they didn't have much money. Television started in Queensland on 1 July 1959 and Grandpa Jack had a television by 1960. Dudley and Joan didn't have a television for another five years—it was a big household investment. Oh, that TV was a source of wonder to Sue-Ellen. It was so exciting to watch it, even just the news or advertisements for Vegemite or a grown-up drink called Porphyry Pearl, but TV watching was carefully rationed to an hour a day, after dinner. There were rumours of dangerous rays from televisions that could make you sick if you watched too much.

Outside the house was Grandpa Jack's toolshed. He used to hang sheets over his tools and seeds on the weekends so that Sue-Ellen could use it as her cubbyhouse. She spent a long time in there, playing house, and then she would go out to inspect Grandpa Jack's veggie garden. His garden was always ordered and productive, with a variety of vegetables, and looked different from the other gardens Sue-Ellen could see through the fence. There were two Greek families on the uphill side, and they grew olives and lemons and long rows of lettuce and tomatoes and corn. Their gardens were big enough to feed the whole neighbourhood. There were mostly Greek families and Irish families on Copeland Street, but it was the Irish family next door that especially captivated Sue-Ellen.

Unlike the houses with neat gardens all around, the Rowlands' house had a rusty car in the backyard, piles of old pipes, and chickens that ran wild. And, most thrilling of all, the garden was full of children. The Rowlands had seven children and they all ran and shouted as much as they wanted to. Sue-Ellen crept closer and closer to the fence to watch them play and sometimes one of them, a girl called Leigh, would call out to her to come over and play.

'Can I, Grandma?' Sue-Ellen would ask.

'No,' Doris would say, firmly. 'You can talk to them through the fence, but you can't go over it.'

Sue-Ellen tried hard to work out the rules of the fence. It wasn't the same at her parents' house. At home they never locked the back door and neighbours often popped in for a cup of tea, fences or no fences.

Grandma Doris never went into the Rowlands' house. She would sometimes go up to the fence and call out, 'Yoo hoo, Mrs Rowland.' And Mrs Rowland would come out, rubbing her hands on her apron, and say 'Yoo hoo' back. Grandma Doris might give her a plate of leftover food for the children or some scraps for the chooks. They would chat pleasantly for a minute or two and then go back into their houses.

On Saturday mornings, before her dad went back home and left her with her grandparents, he would always go down to the fence and talk to Charley Rowland. Sometimes they talked for hours but, however hot the sun was, they never crossed the fence to stand in the shade. They made a funny pair: Dudley neatly dressed in slacks and a white shirt and polished shoes, and Charley in shorts and a singlet. Dudley would never wear shorts unless he was mowing the lawn. To Sue-Ellen's eyes, Charley always looked dirty. He was a railway fettler and his skin had turned dark brown from the sun; his fingers were bright yellow from smoking rollies.

46

'What are they talking about, Grandma?' Sue-Ellen would ask, because kids weren't allowed to join in the conversation between the two men.

'Nothing you'd be interested in,' Doris would say. The long, lazy-looking chat over the fence, punctuated by cigarette rolling and slow skywards looks, might have been a neighbourly chat. But even at age four, Sue-Ellen already knew that when Dad was chatting to people, it was work. They were exchanging information that appeared meaningless to Sue-Ellen but was apparently of value to Charley in his union work and Dad in his ASIO work.

That fence at Copeland Street drew the line between the two men—one a unionist and one a spy; one a Labor man and one a Liberal; one a Catholic and one a Mason. The divisions were clear and seemed eternal but, provided the fence stood between them, there was nothing to stop them being good neighbours.

As well as his random disappearances, her dad was away on the trips he took to regional Queensland every six weeks. When he was away, Joan had a special ritual at dinnertime. She told the children that, when Dad was away, they could ask her anything they liked during dinner and she would answer it. She could only do it when Dad was away, though; when he was there, they had to be quiet, because he was tired after work.

Sue-Ellen wasn't game to ask questions herself because she knew she was the dumb one in the family and she didn't want to get in trouble for asking a stupid question. So she primed Mark to ask questions for her. Mark used to get frustrated that she wouldn't ask herself, but he always ended up doing it for her. At different times, they asked about sex, or gardening, or current affairs, and Joan would always answer their questions honestly. When Sue-Ellen wanted to know what a penis looked like, Mark told her she had to ask Joan herself. Joan told her that they looked like the big beef sausages the family ate. When Sue-Ellen grew up, she was surprised to discover that penises were not freckly.

One night, Sue-Ellen asked Mark to ask why Grandma Doris couldn't visit the Rowlands and why they didn't come into her place to sit down.

'It's because they are a different religion and they have different politics,' said Mum. 'And also they have different roles in life. The Rowlands are working people. So they like each other, but they just don't cross the fence. That would be too close.'

Sue-Ellen wanted to cross that fence. When she visited Grandma Doris, she got closer and closer to the fence and then she started to sit on top of it, legs slung over on the Rowlands' side, watching intently everything the kids were doing. One day, when Leigh called out for her to come over, she cast one quick look about to see if Grandma Doris was watching, and then slid over, quickly and neatly, into forbidden territory.

Leigh was the youngest girl in the Rowland family. She was seven—two years older than Sue-Ellen—but Sue-Ellen was taller. Both the girls had fair hair in plaits; Leigh was chubby, with freckles, while Sue-Ellen was thin. On the day Sue-Ellen answered Leigh's call they became best friends, as close as sisters, and stayed that way for five years, until Leigh went to high school and Sue-Ellen and her family moved to The Gap. Today, Sue-Ellen says Leigh was the best friend she ever had, the only person outside the family who knew her. The not-telling-people-anything aspect of their family meant that it was too tricky to have close friends as she got older. Her only true friend in life came from across that childhood fence.

That first day, Leigh took her hand and they walked into the dim space under the Rowlands' house. The ground was dirt and, before her eyes had adjusted, Sue-Ellen walked into a cobweb and had to pull it out of her hair. Never in her life had she been in a place so dirty and undomesticated. And in the middle of all that ungodly dirt and the smell of damp were great boxes, like treasure chests, full of shining fabric. Box after box of amazing dress-up clothes, from who knows where, were at their disposal. The two girls spent hours that first day, and many others, parading around in beautiful lace gowns and high heels and jewels, playing make-believe. Dressing up was a part of Sue-Ellen's life at home too, but it was dressing up to be invisible. This was dressing up to be strange, fantastic and beautiful. For the first time in her life, in the dust and cob-webs under the Rowlands' house, Sue-Ellen could be whoever she wanted.

They didn't just stay under the house. While Grandma Doris was working at her sewing machine, Leigh took Sue-Ellen out with her around the streets of Milton and taught her new skills, like how to cadge for food. They would go to the back of a cake shop and stand there, looking inside. At first, Sue-Ellen would be ready to introduce herself politely, as she had been taught: 'Hi. I'm Sue-Ellen and this is my friend Leigh.' But

Leigh shushed her quickly. 'Just look sad,' she hissed. The two girls stood there looking sad and it only took a few minutes before someone would hand out a parcel of broken biscuits or some jam doughnuts that hadn't come out quite right.

The football stadium, Lang Park, was just down the hill from where they lived and sometimes the whole Rowland family would walk down to watch a game of rugby league. Sue-Ellen would go with them as a matter of course—nowadays she thinks how kind it was of them to pay for her to go, without any questions, although her family was better off than the Rowlands. While everyone else watched the game and roared at the players, she and Leigh would run around busily collecting empty bottles and putting them in a sack. Later they would take the bottles to the shop because you could get a penny or two for every bottle. They spent all the profits straightaway on lollies.

Grandma Doris didn't exactly change her rules, but she turned a blind eye to Sue-Ellen's flouting of the fence laws. Leigh was welcome in her house as well. Charley Rowland was a contact, so Dad also turned a blind eye to the friendship—although he probably didn't know how freely the girls wandered in the neighbourhood. Often the girls still stuck to the fence line as long as it didn't stop them being together—they walked around the whole neighbourhood on top of the fences, stickybeaking at what the neighbours were doing. There was a fine mulberry tree growing by the fence in one yard and they could eat their fill of mulberries without going into the yard. An old man often came out when he saw them, and they would sit on top of the fence and chat to him about what else they'd seen and done that day. At Grandma Doris's, you could talk to anyone as long as you didn't go into their yard. For example, Sue-Ellen liked to talk to the garbos when they ran in with the bins—something that was strictly forbidden at home.

The glorious climax of every weekend was Sunday afternoon. Grandma Doris rounded up the two dirty, barefoot girls and herded them into her little bathroom, where she had filled the old-fashioned bath with sudsy water. Leigh liked to have her Sunday bath with Sue-Ellen, because at home she had to share the bathwater with six other siblings, and it was always cold and scummy. The girls sat in the bath for hours, sucking a face washer each and giggling like 'eejits'. When they clambered out of the cooling bath, to be rubbed down briskly by Grandma Doris, they would settle in front of the television to eat pikelets for tea and watch their favourite Walt Disney show set in the magical world of Disneyland. As soon as the golden turrets of the Sleeping Beauty castle faded from the screen, Dudley would arrive to take Sue-Ellen home and Leigh would retreat into her over-the-fence world again until the next weekend.

Grandma Doris never let on to Joan and Dudley that Sue-Ellen was leading the life of an urchin with Leigh, and they would have been shocked if they had known. At home, Sue-Ellen was always neat and clean, and she liked being like that. But she also loved being dirty and barefoot with Leigh. She never felt as free as she did with her friend at Copeland Street. They often got into trouble together, but it never seemed to matter too much. At home, when she was noisy or naughty, it felt like she was doing something really bad, but Grandma Doris would just give her a smack on the behind and send her outside.

⌒

Sue-Ellen could accept rules when they were clear and punishments when they were fair. But sometimes the rules were confusing.

During the sixties, there was a popular TV quiz show called *Concentration*. It was a memory game hosted by Philip Brady. Joan's powers of observation and memory made her an expert at memory games, and she went on the show and won a lot of prizes. One of the prizes was a set of men's shirts, which were the wrong size for Dudley.

Joan asked eleven-year-old Sue-Ellen to go into the McDonnell & East department store with the shirts. She was to say that her mother had bought them there but they were the wrong size, and to ask if she could exchange them for shirts of the right size.

Sue-Ellen took the bus into town, found her way to McDonnell & East and, despite being nervous, carried out the shirt deception easily. Elated, she wandered around the department store with all its temptations. The jewellery section was especially alluring, and she found a bracelet there that she wanted to give to her sister. Before she had even thought about it, she had slipped the bracelet into her bag.

The shop detective, who had been watching her, pounced. He marched her to the manager's office and interviewed her. Sue-Ellen made matters worse for herself by answering evasively or not at all. The manager was not on the list so she didn't know if she could tell him the truth. The police were called, and Sue-Ellen was taken home in a squad car.

When the police had gone, Joan sent Sue-Ellen to her room. Sue-Ellen sat waiting, wondering how she could make her knees stop trembling, until both her parents came in. She stood up to face them and they sat on the bed and looked at her with silent judgement. Finally, Joan spoke in an icy voice. 'I don't know why you did that. You have put your father's job in jeopardy.' They got up and walked out of the room.

It was the worst punishment of Sue-Ellen's life. She had disgraced the whole family and put her dad's work at risk. For months, she waited anxiously to hear whether her father had been sacked. But her shame was compounded by bursts of anger, which made her ashamed all over again. Her parents had sent her to do something dishonest and then they were angry with her for shoplifting. She hadn't told the police about the shirts; shouldn't her parents have been grateful?

The rules were supposed to protect them all by making everything clear—distinctly black or distinctly white—but this was confusing. Most children suffer this kind of confusion at some time. Parents make strict rules for their children but break them themselves—like rules about staying up late at night or watching too much TV. Growing up means discovering that we have to work out the rules for ourselves. And Brisbane in the sixties was a conformist town where an appearance of respectability was essential. People survived the conformity by adopting a complex set of double standards until a new rebellious generation swept away the old rules.

But, for the Doherty kids, any confusion about rules was alarming and dangerous. You had to know exactly what to do, and what was right and wrong in every circumstance, or some nameless, terrible thing would happen. Maybe the Russians would come. Maybe her parents would be tortured. Maybe the world would end.

Sue-Ellen was nearly sixty when she first spoke to anyone about that episode from her childhood, and her voice rose an octave as she told the story. She sounded like a frightened child. She had never been able to make sense of the fact that her mother had broken the rules too, but that she was the one who was punished.

6

Flying

Sue-Ellen is flying. Although it is the middle of the night, and everyone thinks she is fast asleep in bed, she is miles away, in the Cut Out. The Cut Out is what they call the piece of land cut out of bushland close to her school at Ashgrove. Even in the daytime, it is a private place between the busy regimentation of school life and the dark tangle of bush. Sometimes children take a short cut across the Cut Out to get to school, but they don't stop there to play. At night, it lies empty and inviting under the starry sky.

Sue-Ellen pads along a kid-made path in bare feet, cool in her summer pyjamas, until she gets to the ridge at the top of the Cut Out. She stands still for a moment, listening to the quiet rustle of the bush. When she lifts her arms above her head, they feel very soft, like gossamer wings. A gentle breeze lifts her into the air. She rises higher and higher over the trees and into the velvety sky. She knows she is safe because a golden cord around her waist tethers her to the ground. She stays upright, swaying a little forward and back, her arms floating effortlessly. Released from gravity, she feels free, happy and safe.

She turns her head to find Dad floating beside her. He looks happy too. There is no need to speak.

At breakfast the next morning she feels extra hungry, eating all her porridge and two pieces of fresh white bread with honey at the little table at the top of the stairs where they eat all their meals. Mum packs their lunches and shooshes them out of the door into the car with Dad in her usual fast, efficient way.

On the way to school, Sue-Ellen sits in the front with Dad; Mark and Amanda read their comic books in the back seat. 'Hey, Dad,' she says. 'We were flying again last night.'

'Were we?' he replies, lifting his eyebrow towards her in a listening way. 'Did we have a good time?'

'Yes, we did.'

'I like it when we fly together,' he says. 'You should take any opportunities that come to you in dreams.'

'Okay,' she says. 'You know, there's never anybody else flying when we're there.'

'That's because they don't believe they can,' he says. 'You and I know that anything is possible.'

If Sue-Ellen didn't get much time with her father in the day, she made up for it with episodes of astral travel in her sleep. At those times, she felt happy to be alone with her dad. When she told him about it, he always acted like it was completely normal.

Dudley and Joan both believed you could remake your life the way you wanted it to be, no matter how terrible your childhood had been. You didn't need to remain poor, desperate and alone. Anything was possible with big dreams, courage and hard work. And anything really meant *anything*—even flying.

Joan and Dudley were different from most slouch-hatted ASIO operatives, who were suspicious of anyone 'not normal'. ASIO agents watched people with alternative lifestyles with suspicion and often contempt. But Joan took up Buddhism, Taoism, and esoteric studies based on the work of mystical writer George Gurdjieff, among other things. She joined Amway at one point because it sold organic produce, at a time when eating organic food was a decidedly fringe activity. The children used to ask her what her religion of the week was. She talked to her plants (and even her cynical offspring couldn't help but notice how green and lush her garden became as it grew).

Dudley was interested in every kind of person in the world. He was just fascinated to know what people were like. Even though he was a warrior against communism, a true believer in the ASIO cause, he was interested in individual communists and wanted to know what made them do what they did. He studied them with curiosity and, in some of them, even found things to like.

ASIO tried to pick agents to suit the job. Intellectuals spied on intellectuals; parents watched P&C members. When ASIO wanted to monitor the Victorian artists' colony Montsalvat, in Eltham, they chose Moya Horowitz, a brilliant pianist with an Eastern European name and exotic, Bohemian looks. She spent more than a decade living among and spying on people in the group headed by artist Justus Jorgensen. She told her daughter Miriam, many years later, that she had very much liked the people at Montsalvat and considered them her friends. Miriam asked her how difficult it had been to spy on her friends, and Moya answered that it was difficult, but she had done it 'for king and country'.

Dudley liked hunting, shooting and fishing and he would have stuck out a mile in an artists' colony. Agents in the Brisbane office didn't have the opportunity to specialise, not in the way that Moya Horowitz did, but Dudley was probably the only bloke in the office who could have been safely sent to cover the meetings of the Brisbane UFO Society.

In the sixties, everyone in Brisbane was talking about UFOs—unidentified flying objects. A Polish-American ufologist called George Adamski had written three best-selling books: *Flying Saucers Have Landed, Inside the Space Ships* and *Flying Saucers Farewell*. Adamski claimed to have met with friendly aliens and taken flights in their spaceships to the Moon and other planets. After the books came out, there were reported sightings of UFOs all over the world, including in Brisbane.

The Brisbane UFO Society used to meet in the quaint nineteenth-century Theosophical Society Building in Spring Hill, and Dudley and Joan attended regularly, walking up the winding staircase with one or more of the children to the wood-panelled meeting room in an atmosphere of hushed excitement. The society investigated suspected UFO sightings and wrote detailed reports of what people believed they had witnessed. Members listened quietly as the reports were gravely read out. Afterwards, there were mutterings about secret dossiers of sightings held by government, and conspiracies to keep information from the public. UFO-spotters were up against the world; as well as conspiracies, they faced scoffing from sceptics and attacks from bitter opponents. All that opposition and conspiracy were part of the fun.

Sometimes the murmuring would break out into vigorous debates about intergalactic relations. Members disagreed about the best ways to get acquainted with visitors from other planets, and about whether aliens had friendly intentions or were coming to conquer them.

The Doherty children were caught up in the excitement and pored over the photographs Adamski claimed were of flying saucers, and of the great spaceships from which the saucers—scout ships—were launched. They eagerly scanned the night skies for aliens and discussed what they would do if they were approached by a Venutian ambassador to go with them to the mothership. They also practised mind reading on each other. Languages, mind reading and observation were special talents in the Doherty family, so they had no doubt they would soon be chatting away happily with people from Venus and Saturn, at the very least, and bringing back detailed accounts to Earth of the life on other planets to help the Earthian government.

Did Dudley and Joan believe in UFOs? Quite possibly. They both loved exploring new ideas and new worlds, and they entered into the world of intergalactic conspiracy with gusto. Later the kids joked that their parents had been looking for communists in outer space. But Dudley's job was to infiltrate groups and to report back to ASIO on anything odd or incon-sistent that he had witnessed. Perhaps he was just a rational man who took an interest in any group getting media attention and figured out ways to get to know the key players in that group.

Whatever the downsides of being an ASIO kid, the Doherty kids had more varied and surprising lives than other kids in their neighbourhood. And Sue-Ellen never really stopped believing that she could fly.

PART 2

SUE-ELLEN

7

The Girl Who Came to Stay

Sydney, September 1973

'Why have you taken the phone off the hook?' Sue-Ellen asked Lorraine while they drank their morning coffee at a dented antique table in a terrace house in Glebe.

'Because people are talking about you and my husband, darling, and I'm sick of it,' said Lorraine.

'Really? Before breakfast? What are they saying?'

'They want to know how to get a pants suit like the one that the beautiful blonde wore to the Sydney Opera House last night,' said Lorraine. 'The beautiful blonde who was there with Erich.'

Erich Saikovski had attended the triumphant opening concert of the Sydney Opera House with Sue-Ellen on his arm, knowing she would be good publicity for his fashionable design business. She wore an absinthe-green, raw silk pants suit with padded shoulders. A pants suit was a daring choice for any formal event, and a shocking one for Sydney's biggest social event of the year, but Sue-Ellen had carried it off with panache.

Risk was in the air and the Opera House was the perfect symbol of that. The doomsayers had been calling the building a white elephant for years, but the new words for it in the media were now 'daring', 'dramatic' and 'innovative'.

The prime minister Gough Whitlam and his wife Margaret had been there for the opening performance—Wagner, featuring Swedish soprano Birgit Nilsson and the Sydney Symphony Orchestra. Queen Elizabeth would open the Opera House officially in another month, ensuring its acceptance in respectable circles, but its first concert was a celebration of Gough's new Australia. As well as ushering in equal pay for women and the end of conscription, the Whitlam government had broken with tradition by choosing to support the arts. Finally, Australians could take opera and theatre as seriously as football and cricket—if they dared. And Sue-Ellen dared.

'It's lucky I adore you,' said Lorraine, pouring coffee out of a blue-and-white patterned pot with one hand, while holding baby Aaron, usually known as Dweezel, under her other arm. 'At the jazz club tonight, everyone will be looking at us out of the corner of their eyes and wondering about us.'

'As if you'd care what anyone thought,' said Sue-Ellen affectionately. 'I am so lucky to have found you and Erich and Dweezel. You are my family now. Even your spooky black cat is my family.'

'We love having you. And Baroushka is not spooky; she's just sensitive.'

Sue-Ellen was twenty years old. She had arrived at the Saikovski house a year earlier when she had come to Sydney for a holiday. She had come with an introduction from a hairdresser called Bruce—an old friend of Erich and Lorraine's. They knew Bruce wouldn't send them someone who didn't interest them, and they instantly saw the potential for fun in the striking girl with her provincial clothes. They insisted on her staying with them for her holidays and, before long, she had become a long-term tenant. No one who had experienced Sydney with Erich and Lorraine would be content to go back to Brisbane.

Erich had grown up in a German family in Cairns. He had had a rough childhood and the scars had stayed with him. He was accidentally shot in the face by a school friend with a bow and arrow and ended up with a glass eye. At the age of fifteen he was sexually attacked by a man who had interviewed him for a job, along with two of the man's friends who had suddenly appeared during the interview. After that, Erich developed a stammer that stayed with him for life. As a German in country Queensland, he was always an outsider. He grew into a tall, gentle man with a flamboyant manner, and he made the most beautiful clothes Sue-Ellen had ever seen. At first sight she had assumed he was gay, until she discovered he was happily and dotingly married to Lorraine.

In those days, blondes were stereotyped as dumb and Lorraine fooled most of the people most of the time. Sue-Ellen, another blonde who noticed things, soon worked out that Lorraine was the brains of the family—a tough, shrewd bargainer with an eye for making money in unlikely ways. For instance, in the days when synthetic fabrics ruled, she would buy faded linen fabrics for a couple of dollars each from the markets, restore them to their original beauty and sell them for large sums to fashionable people who cared about quality. She also had fascinating, way-out beliefs. She loved heavy metal music as much as jazz and she did crystal divining and studied the I Ching. For all her toughness and strangeness, Lorraine mothered Sue-Ellen, and Sue-Ellen felt at ease with her.

Sue-Ellen had brought her much-thumbed bankbook from Brisbane, a faithful record of careful savings. Within a fortnight, she had blown every cent on clothes. Erich introduced her to clothes of silk and crepe de chine in styles she had never imagined. She was an actress and had done some modelling work in Brisbane—she had a magnificent figure and she knew how to walk. All she needed was the clothes to set it off.

Sue-Ellen had known from childhood that if you wanted to fit into a new world, the first step was to wear the right clothes. Her new world was the world of high fashion, the world of nothing-but-the-best. She had the looks, but she didn't have the budget. Luckily, she had the right friends.

Erich enjoyed helping her to find her own bold and provocative look, with feathers, chains, velvet and tall shoes—fashions inspired by tough, chic Paris designers like Thierry Mugler and Claude Montana, but adapted for Australia's heat and casual style.

'I'll make you a deal, darling,' Erich told Sue-Ellen. 'You pick out the materials you want for your clothes and I will let you use my patterns.' Erich's designs were only worn by Sydney's A-listers, so this was a generous offer.

'Oh Erich, I love you forever. Do you think my cutting skills are good enough for your pieces?'

'No,' he said firmly. 'My staff will cut them for you, but you can do the sewing. And Lorraine will take you shopping. We're not going to let you just go to a department store and buy whatever ghastly materials they offer you.'

Lorraine introduced Sue-Ellen to a kind of shopping she had never experienced. Every weekend they travelled together to country towns by bus and train to explore old-fashioned haberdasheries, where old stock of fine materials could be bought at budget prices. Lorraine showed her how to feel the quality in a cloth and how to be bold without being garish. In the city, she introduced her to budget outlets for expensive shoes. If she bought classic shoes or ones that emphasised particular features of her clothes, no one would ever notice they were last season's styles.

Sue-Ellen found a job working the night shift on reception at the Travelodge at Rushcutters Bay in the city's east. She slept briefly in the mornings and, for the rest of her days and weekend nights, she threw herself into life in the big smoke. Dressed to dazzle, Sue-Ellen was soon going to theatres, concerts, shows and restaurants with the most amusing people in Sydney's art, theatre and fashion worlds, often escorted by Erich, who needed to be seen at those events, while Lorraine stayed home happily with Dweezel.

People raised their eyebrows at seeing the beautiful, vivacious girl on the arm of the successful designer, but there was never anything in it. Erich and Lorraine were devoted to each other and Sue-Ellen was their mutual project. On Saturdays,

Lorraine went shopping at the markets and brought back delicious ingredients that the other two cooked. They shared the cleaning agreeably, played with the baby, and laughed and talked about art and fashion, music and theatre. On the weekends they had dinner parties using their 1930s cutlery and dinnerware, which was a style that matched the furniture and paintings. Sue-Ellen heard from several people that Erich's collection of Clarice Cliff ceramics was the best in Australia. She loved going on jaunts with them both to city markets or little country junk shops, where they hunted for Art Deco pottery, linens and old lace. She felt sophisticated and daring as she trawled for treasure among the trash—in her Brisbane life she had thought secondhand clothes were just for poor people.

Sydney was so much fun. In Sydney, she could wear mustard yellow or Yves Klein blue, or whatever she damn well felt like. She could say whatever she liked and no one cared. She went to chic jazz clubs, swam on Sydney beaches in teeny bikinis and strutted like a diva. She was a gorgeous showpiece, in love with life. She had everything she needed—except a man.

She would have liked to meet a nice, hunky man, but she was sure it wasn't going to be the bloke who invaded their living room one Sunday morning, when the little family was recovering companionably from a big night in the Sydney clubs. Sue-Ellen was flicking through copies of *Vogue* when a tall man strolled in, followed by a big red setter dog. With his bushy beard and long black curly hair, he looked as if he hadn't washed for a day or two at least. He wore dirty jeans with an old tartan shirt that had a rip in the pocket. Sue-Ellen looked at Erich and Lorraine for guidance, but they were offering

Dweezel cold teething rings and making soothing baby noises, and they took no notice of the new arrival. She kept reading, appearing not to notice the man and his dog. After a while, he picked up a women's magazine and read it from front to back, apparently with deep interest. When he finished the magazine, he put it down, stood up, stretched noisily and walked out again.

Sue-Ellen waited until the front door had closed behind him before she started to shriek.

'Who on earth was that? Did you know that guy?'

Lorraine and Erich looked up, surprised. 'That was Hugh,' said Erich.

'Well, what was he doing?'

'He was just visiting.'

'Really! That's a funny way to visit. I thought he was a homeless guy who had just wandered in.'

She must have exclaimed too much. Lorraine looked at her with a keen glance and changed the topic quietly. Then, a few days later, she announced that they were all going out to dinner at a new Italian place in Glebe and their friend Hugh was going to join them. Sue-Ellen was less than impressed, especially when Erich and Lorraine dropped out at the last minute because the baby had a temperature. She said she would stay home too, but they insisted she keep the rendezvous with Hugh.

'Poor homeless guy. This is a treat and we can't let him down,' said Lorraine. Sue-Ellen sniffed but she kept the date with Hugh at the dim restaurant with its gingham tablecloths and its candles in empty Mateus bottles with wax dripping down the glass.

It was suddenly obvious that Hugh, wearing clean, very tight jeans and with his curly hair brushed and shiny, was a good-looking guy. *Very* good-looking. He talked easily, drawing Sue-Ellen out. He was doing an apprenticeship as a jeweller and he commented appreciatively on the setting of her dramatic stone earrings. He also suggested other shapes that might suit her face. This fashion talk was easy, but Hugh had other topics that were new to her. Like politics.

'What do you want to be after the revolution?' he grinned at her.

'What revolution?' she said, wide-eyed.

'You've missed it?' he quizzed her. 'Didn't you notice everything was changing? That everyone can get a free education now and free health care, and that no one can be sent off to fight foreign wars on the roll of a dice in a lottery?'

'Oh, politics,' she said. 'I'm not really interested in politics.'

'Why not?'

'There was too much of it in my house, growing up,' she said, and refused to say any more.

She listened to him though and enjoyed his sense of idealism and hope, his belief in the power to change the world for the better. Was he deluded? Probably. Her dad would have been sure of it. But it was a cheering delusion.

Another weird thing about Hugh was that he listened to her as though he really wanted to know what she thought. She was used to having boys show off to her. One rainy evening she counted up that she had gone out with 180 different boys and they usually only lasted for one or two dates. Mesmerised by her breasts and her glamour, the boys would try to win her interest over unaccustomed dinners at white-tablecloth restaurants they could barely afford. None of them ever tried to get past her vivacious manner to find out what she really thought and felt. They talked earnestly about music and football and cars, mistaking her polite manners for interest, and it didn't take long for them to bore her stiff.

When she was nineteen, Sue-Ellen's mother had arranged for her to be deflowered. It was part of the big change in Joan that had happened after Dudley died. (Or disappeared, as Sue-Ellen still thought of it.) For most of Sue-Ellen's life, Joan had strongly disapproved of pre-marital sex. So much so that Sue-Ellen had understood that virginity until marriage was one of the unbreakable family rules. But, in the seventies, Joan had changed her mind. She said it was better to try before you buy, and she arranged the whole thing. She invited a boy, an old friend of Sue-Ellen's, to come over and visit one night when Mark had moved out and Amanda was away. It was winter; Joan lit the fire and put on some low, bluesy music on the record player. She poured Sue-Ellen and the boy a glass of wine, laid out some angels-on-horseback and Jatz with cheese, and then announced that she was going out with a friend and not to expect her back that night.

The nice boy was expecting this—he had been briefed on his mission. Sue-Ellen had not. But her mother knew her well, knew her need to appear grown-up and in control, and believed it was the best thing for her. Sue-Ellen politely gave up her virginity and continued going out with that boy in a companionably sexy relationship for the next year, until she left for Sydney. They had a lot of fun, and she was fond of him.

They went out with friends, danced and listened to music, went to the theatre. She picked what they did, and he went along. If she wanted a night alone, he accepted it. He wasn't particularly interested in her ideas and opinions, and at the time that had suited her. She had found it safer all her life not to have any ideas and opinions.

So it was disturbing to find that Hugh was inquisitive about her and the kind of person she was. He asked about her family and noticed that he didn't get very far with that line of questioning.

'What did your dad do?' he asked.

'Just something boring for the government. I don't really know,' she lied, giving him her 'blue-eyed bimbo' look and leaning forward to give him a glimpse of cleavage.

'Right,' said Hugh in his lazy, amused style. He clocked the cleavage with interest and let her bat away the question, but she never knew when he might drop another into the conversation, from a different angle, even when they were deep in wine and flirtation. The nice boys had been happy to take any version of herself she offered, but Hugh was ready to challenge any 'bullshit' she offered him. She was the mistress of deception and evasion, but she suspected that Hugh was onto her.

After dinner, Hugh walked her home. She paused to kiss him goodnight at the door of the darkened house—standard first-date routine. He ignored her uplifted face, pushed the door open and walked her to the wooden staircase. He put his hand low around her waist as they walked up the shadowy stairs and kept his eyes on her face. Halfway up, she baulked.

'Hey, what are you doing? I didn't ask you up to my room.'

Hugh looked at her steadily. 'I'm not playing that game,' he said. 'I don't want a platonic relationship. If you want me, get your gear off. If not, you won't see me again.'

This was not in the script. Sue-Ellen was used to being in control. None of her boys had ever laid down the law. But she felt her nipples harden instantly—annoyingly, her body had been waiting for a man who didn't take directions. She took her gear off.

Six weeks later she moved out of Erich and Lorraine's house. Hugh moved out of his share house and they rented a tiny one-bed apartment in Paddington, just east of the city—a perfect love nest.

She was wildly happy—and shocked to the core. Despite her mother's efficient arrangement of her first sexual encounter, she had grown up with 100 per cent certainty that she would not live with a man until he put a diamond on her finger. This new life with Hugh was impossible and irresistible and she didn't know herself.

'You were such a prude when you came to us,' said Lorraine, teasing.

'And now you are a scarlet woman,' said Erich.

'I know,' said Sue-Ellen. 'This is not what I want to do but it's out of my control. I just have to do it.'

She wrote long chatty letters home every week and spent a whole day on the letter in which she explained her change of address. She half expected that her mother would appear on a thunderbolt to stop it happening, but Joan wrote back in a pleasant, encouraging way, asking what she needed in her new kitchen. It was more shocking than if she'd been angry.

'Do you know my mother didn't even care?' she asked Lorraine, as they peeled vegetables for dinner one night.

'That's good. Here, use the peeler—it works better than that knife.'

'But Lorraine—did you hear me? She doesn't care.' Sue-Ellen stopped work to stare at Lorraine. 'In the past year or two she's just got so weird. She arranged for me to lose my virginity and now she wants me to live with a man.'

'She's just moving with the times. Be grateful,' said Lorraine. 'What do you want her to say? "Don't darken my door again"?'

'No'. Sue-Ellen stared out the window to try to work out why she felt so scared. 'But it's like she doesn't want me to come home again. Who's going to protect me now?'

'Who do you think?' asked Lorraine, looking up.

'Hugh?' said Sue-Ellen, uncertainly. 'But I don't know if I can ever trust a man. Especially someone as good looking as Hugh.'

'Okay. Maybe you'll have to start looking after yourself then,' said Lorraine, wiping her hands and placing them on the girl's shoulders. 'Women are doing it for themselves these days,' she quipped, looking her full in the eyes.

'Yeah, I suppose so,' Sue-Ellen said thoughtfully.

'And, also, Hugh's a good man. We've known him forever. Why can't you trust him?'

'I want to. I love him to bits. But he's so good looking and so charming. He's sure to be unfaithful. If I put my life in his hands, I don't want to wake up in the morning and find he has just disappeared.'

Sue-Ellen couldn't work out why she felt so torn about throwing in her lot with Hugh. She adored him, he adored her, and everyone was happy for her. But she felt uneasy at the idea of giving her life over to a man, as though that would be breaking a sacred promise. Walking to Circular Quay one day, enjoying the shine of the harbour and the bustle of boats, she remembered that she *had* made a promise—to herself. She had sworn to wait for her dad.

She was the only one who hadn't believed his cover story about dying, so she was the only one who could help him on whatever mission he was on. And she never broke her promises. How could she help him if she was living in Sydney? And what would he think of her living with a man before marriage anyway? He hadn't got with Mum's new program, which started after he had gone, and he would be so shocked.

Sue-Ellen always pretended to believe her father was dead and, most of the time, the pretence was as good as the truth. But that locked-away part of her had never given up on him and it was making her sweat now. If only she could talk about it to someone! But they had all been sworn to secrecy after Dad had disappeared. Another unbreakable promise.

The more she thought about it, the more ashamed and uncertain she felt. Then another emotion started to cramp her solar plexus: suspicion. If her father was alive, did he really expect her to give up her love, her life, to wait for him? Was he really the great hero she had always believed? Some sneaky memories arose that suggested he wasn't such a shining idol. For example, there were those times with the oysters.

8

Oysters

Dad steers the Holden quickly into a parking spot on Coronation Drive, outside a row of dilapidated nineteenth-century brick terraces. 'I just need to drop in here for a few minutes,' he calls cheerfully to Joan and the kids. He is already out of the car, holding the box of oysters he has bought at the fisho.

Sue-Ellen, sitting in the back on the sweaty vinyl bench seat between Mark and Amanda, starts to wail: 'You said we were going to the park!' Mum gives her the look, the one that would silence a fire engine on the way to a fire. Dad doesn't even answer. He is already across the footpath, walking up the short stone staircase to the front door of one of the terrace houses.

Dad is hardly ever home; he is always working. Sue-Ellen knows Dad has to work very hard because the communists are trying to take over the world and he is one of the people who has to stop them. So he hardly ever takes them to the park, and even when he does, they can never just go to the park. There is always some work thing he has to do on the way. If he goes into the terrace house on Coronation Drive *carrying oysters, Sue-Ellen knows it could be twenty minutes or it could be three hours.*

Mark and Amanda know the drill. They pull out their comic books and start to read, but Sue-Ellen hates reading. Mum is no company either. She just sits there quietly, all ladylike, with her hands folded on her leather handbag, staring out the window till Dad gets back. Sue-Ellen fumes, but she knows she will have to keep quiet or the treat will be called off. She sits very still and memorises the numberplates of all the cars on the street. That will please her dad when he comes out.

Of course, they won't ask Dad what he has been doing in there. You are never allowed to ask Dad where he is going, or who he has been with, or what he is doing. That is strictly forbidden. But if you do just ask it anyway, which Sue-Ellen sometimes does, Mum will just say he is 'working'.

Dudley was a great guy. Anyone would tell you that. In the years after he 'disappeared', Sue-Ellen asked everyone who knew him what he was like. They all said the same things. 'Oh my god, he was so generous'; 'He was so funny'; 'He listened to me when no one else would.' When these people were out of work, he'd come to visit and afterwards they'd open the fridge and find it full of food and wine. Or he'd spend hours helping someone fill in forms because their English wasn't too good. He always had time and answers for the new espionage recruits and, when they were hungry or perplexed, he brought them home to be fed in Joan's comforting kitchen. Strangers liked him straightaway, but Sue-Ellen knew that being likeable had been his job. She was interested in the opinions of the people who knew him best. After she fell in love with Hugh, it started to bother her that she didn't know much about her father.

Sue-Ellen wasn't asking questions about her dad because she doubted his lovability. Even though she had always been in trouble when she was a kid, and Dad had used the strap on her, she had adored him—and she adored him still. She and Mark and Amanda had always known that he was the man to turn to when there was a problem. The world was a dangerous, scary place but, when Dad was around, they were safe. He didn't have a lot of time to spend with his children, and most of that time they were working but, if he gave you his attention, even for a minute or two, you felt ten feet tall. He made you feel like you mattered, and that life was full of exciting possibilities. And Sue-Ellen still believed she was his favourite. (She didn't find out until she was grown up that Amanda and Mark had both felt that too.) If Dudley had asked Sue-Ellen to walk on burning coals, she would have done it without a second's hesitation—but, of course, he never did.

He had loved his kids, but he had loved Mum best. Well, he loved work best, and then Mum, and then them. As kids, they were used to making a noise before they opened a door because they never knew when they would find Dad and Mum smooching or Dad with his hands up Mum's blouse. He couldn't keep his hands off his wife and he always noticed what she wore and how she smelled. Sue-Ellen thought all married couples were like that—romantic and sexy and liking nothing better than to tell the story of how they met. They both loved to say how they were meant for each other and that they would never part.

Everybody had loved Dudley, and yet Sue-Ellen still had these niggling doubts. She had found out by then that the building her father visited on Coronation Drive, carrying oysters, was a brothel. She knew it as a fact, but she couldn't make sense of it. She went to her mum and asked her.

'Why would Dad have been going into a brothel?'

'Think about who goes into brothels,' her mum said. Joan liked Sue-Ellen to work things out herself.

'Men.'

'What kind of men?'

'I don't know, Mum. All kinds of men, I suppose.'

'Yes, all kinds. Including politicians. And lots of visitors to the city go to brothels. They were great sources of information for your father in his work for ASIO.'

'So, Mum . . .'

'Yes, Sue-Ellen.'

'Mum, do you reckon that while he was in there, he said, "While I'm here . . ."?'

'I'd have to be a fool to think he didn't,' said Mum.

Sue-Ellen adored her dad, but she couldn't help thinking about him inside that brothel, enjoying himself with prostitutes, while his wife and children waited outside. What kind of a man would do that? Wasn't that immoral? Wasn't it cruel to her mother? What kind of a man was her father really?

'There had been other women as well. When Sue-Ellen was sixteen, she had heard her mother crying about one of them, someone called Maria. At the time, she couldn't take it in. Her parents were strictly opposed to extra-marital sex, or so they said. It just didn't make sense that her father might have been unfaithful to her mother. She put that information swiftly in the box with all the other things she didn't understand and closed the lid hard. That had worked for a long time, but now the secrets were pressing up against the lid, pushing it open a bit at a time.

The trouble was that work was mixed up with everything. Dad was away so often and that was 'work', but how did they know what he was doing? He could have been doing anything at all.

She found herself wondering about those Christmas cards that came every year from Dad's friend Abe and his wife Doreen in Sydney. They were nice cards with snow and robins and angels and a warm cheery message inside—nothing to worry about, on the face of it. Joan always put Abe's card front and centre on the good dresser, with the other cards. Abe was Dad's best friend from forever, and he and Doreen were Mum and Dad's closest couple friends, even though they didn't see each other as much since the Dohertys had moved to Brisbane. Mum and Dad sometimes went down to Sydney to stay with them, especially when one of Abe's clubs featured a big-time American singer. Once they even saw Frank Sinatra singing, from the best table in the house, as Abe's guest. Abe paid for these treats to thank Dad because Dad was a trained bookkeeper and, every year, he went down for a few days and helped Abe do his stocktake. It was hard work and he always came back exhausted.

Abe and Doreen occasionally came up from Sydney for a visit, when Abe had meetings in Brisbane with nightclub owners he did business with. They stayed in a fancy hotel in town,

but they always came out to The Gap for one of Joan's tasty
roast dinners. Abe was a bit of a joker, friendly and dry, with
a comb-over that the kids giggled about. Doreen was pretty
and kind and she liked to gossip about family and clothes with
Joan while Sue-Ellen listened. Sue-Ellen always asked Doreen
for the story of her wedding to Abe in the Great Synagogue
in Sydney.

Doreen had worn the most unusual wedding dress: a great
hooped gown of fringed silk caught up with silver bows to
reveal an underskirt of silver lamé. She had a giant bouquet of
gardenias and lilies-of-the-valley. Afterwards she and Abe had
a reception for 130 people at the fashionable Savarin restaurant.
And that wasn't all! That same evening, they hosted a cabaret
supper at Abe's club, the Roosevelt, for 400 people, and Doreen
changed into her going-away ensemble of grey and cherry
figured silk that showed off her tiny waist. This dazzling wedding had taken place in 1947 and, although Abe and Doreen
just seemed like an ordinary couple when they came to visit,
they always had an air of unspeakable romance to Sue-Ellen.

Later on, it was hard to connect the ordinary Abe and
Doreen, or even the romantic Abe and Doreen, with what the
newspapers said about Abe Saffron.

When she was a kid, Sue-Ellen just accepted that things
didn't make sense. All three kids did that. Dad might mix with
criminals and villains but that was 'work'. You had to accept it
and not ask questions, even of yourself. Sue-Ellen was so good
at keeping questions and doubts locked away that she didn't
even know she had any.

But when she fell in love with Hugh, those questions started bursting out of the box. Suddenly she couldn't help wondering what it actually meant that Abe Saffron was Dad's best friend and that Dad took oysters to visit brothels. Who *was* her father, really?

She couldn't talk to anyone about it, but she became unusually quiet and reflective. Once Hugh snapped his fingers and asked, 'Where do you go to, my lovely?' She laughed and said she was trying to decide whether to buy the vintage Dior frock she had found in an op shop. Actually, she had been reviewing the lives of her parents, trying to look at them as an adult would look at them, assessing them as a stranger would.

9

Bastard Child

Some people thought of Dudley Doherty as the man with everything—a beautiful home and family, and a job that gave him freedom to do whatever he wanted, no questions asked. Dudley thought that too. He was in love with his life, and believed he could have anything he wanted, provided he worked for it. He didn't know he was part of the last generation of men who thought they could have it all. But he never forgot that he started out in life with nothing.

Dudley's mum, Doris, was a lively, warm-hearted woman from a prosperous family. Her father was a gold mine manager on the rich fields of Lucknow, near Orange, and she grew up in a big, comfortable house in the nearby country town of Millthorpe, with a maid to help her mother with the housework. Doris's mother, Amy, loved her two boys but had no interest in Doris and her sister. She didn't want those girls under her feet, and she made her feelings known. So, when twenty-one-year-old Doris, with her long red hair, white skin and dusting of freckles discovered she was pregnant to handsome Clifford Doherty from Sydney town, she needed to marry him. Her mum didn't want her. Anyway, she was in love with him.

Surprisingly for a bloke who wasn't exactly the settling-down type, Cliff popped the question. He probably thought he was onto a good thing marrying the daughter of the manager of a gold mine but, if so, he got that wrong. There were no handouts from Amy, whatever her husband may have wanted to do. Amy never gave away anything, especially not to the daughters she despised.

Doris may have been happy with Cliff Doherty for a little while, setting up their house in the rural town of Walgett, in northern New South Wales, while she waited dreamily for her baby. We don't know what Cliff did for a living, but we know from Joan and Sue-Ellen, who heard it from Doris, that it wasn't long before he started stealing the housekeeping money out of the tin on the mantelpiece and spending it on drinking and gambling. Then he used it to buy cheap presents for other girls. Doris was easygoing, but when she heard that the girl at the fish and chip shop had a dear little new baby and that Cliff Doherty was the father, she gave up on her husband as a bad job. She took the last of the change off the mantelpiece, tied up her few belongings in an old shawl, locked the front door for the last time and went to the train station with Dudley. She would ask her mother for help. It would be hard to do, but there was nowhere else to go.

By that time, Amy Dean was a widow living comfortably in a terrace house in Glebe. All her children had grown up and left, and they mostly didn't talk to her anymore because it never brought anything good. She had been cruel to the girls, and even the favoured boys didn't like spending time with her once they grew up and found out how she had set the four children against each other.

But Dudley was a delicious baby and Amy Dean wanted him as soon as she saw him. She made a deal with Doris: she would look after Dudley as long as Doris got a job and sent her money each week for his keep. There were very few jobs for women in 1923, and the only way Doris could earn a living was to go west and work as a cook on a station. She was a good cook and an accomplished dressmaker, so she had no trouble getting a place on a rural property where domestic skills were highly valued. She kissed her baby goodbye and went west. Every year she got one week off; she would go to Sydney and visit her little boy as he grew up in the home of a woman who resented Doris's very existence.

At least Doris knew that Dudley was well fed and cared for at his grandmother's house—and doted on as well. But Dudley grew up knowing that he owed his grandmother, big time, for playing the role of both father and mother to him. Amy Dean saw Dudley as her personal property; he was not Doris's child, and he was not even his own person. He belonged to Amy and she expected total loyalty and obedience.

So when Dudley, as a child, started roaming the Sydney streets in the daytime with his cousin John, Amy called him to heel pretty fast. 'Don't forget you are a bastard child of a filthy two-timer and you would have died on the streets without me,' said Amy, spitting at him in her anger. In fact, Dudley thought he was a bastard, a child born out of wedlock, until his grandmother died, on Christmas Eve in 1960. He found his birth certificate among her papers and realised that his parents had been married at the time of his birth.

Yet until she died, Dudley believed that his grandmother was his great benefactor, that she had rescued him from disgrace, and that no price was too high to pay for her interest in him. When he got his first job, he naturally gave his wage to his grandmother. He saw it as his duty to pay for Amy Dean's keep and to take care of her, and he always did it handsomely. But he didn't forget his own mother either, much as his grandmother would have liked him to. He was a loyal and affectionate child and he loved his mum. When Doris came to visit, so lovely and so kind, she told him they would be together again one day and for many years he waited patiently for that time to come.

He was a promising student, apparently well set up for a good steady job, one that would allow him to take care of his grandmother and maybe start a family of his own one day, in a home where his mother would be welcome. He studied hard at school, and his teachers expected him to matriculate, then go on to further study and become an accountant.

Ten days before his matric exam, Dudley stepped off a tram on the wrong side, eagerly following cousin John, his boyhood hero. He lost more than his leg that day: John didn't even come back to find out what happened to him, to see his shocking pain and the pool of blood. Afterwards Dudley lay in hospital, bleeding and frightened, sure that he could never sit that exam. The steady office job he had counted on was suddenly an impossible dream. It was 1938, the memory of the Great Depression was still fresh for most Australians, and there was still a sense that only the fittest and strongest flourished.

It must have been a hospital visiting scheme that brought Dudley in touch with Brigadier Johns from the Salvation Army, a visit that changed the course of his life forever. The Salvation Army—a British-born 'army of Christian soldiers'—had started its Australian existence in 1880 when Edward Saunders stood on the back of a greengrocer's cart in Adelaide's Botanic Park to give a rousing sermon. But it seemed that these preachers weren't only interested in souls—they cared for bodies too. 'If there's a man here who hasn't had a square meal today, let him come home to tea with me,' said another of the early Australian Salvationists, John Gore. No wonder the Salvos became a popular movement all over Australia, famous for their soup kitchens as well as their morals, aiming to help people without discrimination wherever there was hardship or injustice. They helped the poor before the government thought of providing pensions, and they were active during the Depression.

The family has no records now of Brigadier Johns, only a sense of gratitude and regard that has been handed down through three generations. They don't know his full name or what he looked like or many details of what he did for Dudley. But, as Dudley told the story, the Brigadier gave him the courage and support to sit for his matriculation exam ten days after the accident, as soon as he left the hospital, despite the shock and pain he was still suffering.

And, when he passed the exams, Dudley said that the Brigadier stayed in his life to help him find work and to support him through his part-time accountancy studies. Dudley said he could not have managed all that without him. The Salvos became a kind of extended family for a boy who was short on loving family members. They taught him the sacred duty of feeding people and they taught him that everyone deserved kindness. Dudley even joined the Salvation Army band, playing his euphonium in the church or on street corners to proclaim his hope and faith.

The warmth of Salvation Army life may have been the origin of Dudley's ambition to join the Australian armed services. When World War II began, he tried to enlist. He was refused—the army did not hire one-legged men. But Dudley was never a bloke to take no for an answer and he desperately wanted to serve his country. He kept applying until his persistence paid off, and he won a job in Supply. On 23 October 1941, he was sent to the 5th Base Ordnance Depot at Moorebank, south-west Sydney, and put in charge of firearms. In 1945 he was promoted to warrant officer second class and he stayed working at the army depot, even after the war, until 1948.

The attractions at Moorebank were diverse. Apart from an outlet for Dudley's genuine patriotism, it offered a secure job, mates, and the nearby bush village of Liverpool where a family of pretty girls called Ridgway lived. The Ridgway house was a magnet for a group of soldiers and staff working at the army base. As well as raising beautiful girls, Leah and Harry

Ridgway grew fruit and vegetables, and they had a cow called Ginger for milk. When one of the older girls brought a man home, he always had a good meal and a bowl of homemade ice cream, and he would go back to the base with a package of fluffy scones.

Bettina, the second-oldest girl, had a boyfriend she often brought home for tea, and one night she and her boy-friend brought Dudley Doherty with them. He was tall, handsome and charming, and Bettina thought he would be a great match for gentle Clair. Dudley was easy and comfortable with the whole family and he soon became a regular visitor. But he didn't come for the ice cream and he didn't come for Clair either. The one he had his eye on was sixteen-year-old Joan, the plucky youngest daughter with the long legs who milked the cows, chopped wood for the fires and fought the kids at school who picked on her beloved big sister Clair.

Joan took a job at the army base as a telephonist, at the same depot as Dudley. She liked to see him about, unaware that he was changing his routes to be close to her. Maybe Dudley developed his famous charm to camouflage the fact that he was a poor, one-legged, fatherless boy who had nothing in the world but his great hopes and dreams. Whatever disad-vantages he saw in himself, his way of attending to people as though they were the only people in the world meant that he was always attractive to women. Joan was physically strong and capable, and a fighter, but she was still an inexperienced girl from the bush, and she didn't stand a chance against the Doherty charm. Dudley was serious. He was in love, and he said there was nothing he could do about it. He had washed up on Joan's shore and she had to take him in, he said.

He invited her to the Milperra Ball at the army depot, the big social event of the year. She accepted shyly and borrowed a dress from one of her sisters. Dudley got staggeringly drunk at the ball and one of his friends had to take Joan home afterwards. It made no difference to Joan. By that time, she had made up her mind. Dudley was the love of her life and nothing would ever change that.

After the ball, they began dating. He took her to the movies or they went shooting. Dudley was a good shot, and Joan's father had taught her to use a rifle too. They competed against each other, shooting at targets. He got mad when she beat him, which made her laugh. They were together every moment they were free, and they talked endlessly. They told each other secrets, things they had never told anyone before. Dudley swore he would always protect her.

But it took a long time for him to propose—four years. Joan knew it was because of his grandmother. Dudley explained how his dad had been a bad 'un and had left him and his mum, and how she'd had to leave him with his grandmother while she went to work out west. Now his mum, Doris, had married a kind and loyal man called Jack, whose only fault was a weakness for gambling. Doris and Jack lived in Brisbane, so Dudley had taken over the support of his grandmother. It would be hard for him to take on a wife as well. He never said a word against his grandmother but, after a while, it became obvious to Joan that Amy Dean didn't plan on sharing Dudley with anyone.

Dudley would find a way though. He always had a dream and a plan, and he told Joan everything in his heart. He had learned some good skills with guns in the army and he wanted to put them to use in his own business. He and a friend decided to start a gunsmithing business in Wagga Wagga, a small military town on the banks of the Murrumbidgee. Joan was a dreamer too, and Wagga Wagga (the Wiradjuri name for 'place of many crows') was not part of her dream. She wanted city life, and a home of her own with a garden, and she wanted to study and become a doctor. She had always known she was clever, even though she had had to leave school very young to work.

One evening in 1948, she was helping Dudley to glue the stocks on rifles for his business. She didn't like that business and she didn't want to go to Wagga Wagga, and she didn't even know if he was going to take her, but she always helped him with all his plans.

'I'd like your advice, Jo Jo,' he said, as he looked down the barrel of a rifle.

She looked at him, glad to be asked, hoping it was something she knew about.

'I've had a job offer in Sydney. Something a bit secret.'

As they worked side by side, he told her that a new organisation called ASIO was looking for recruits and he had been offered a job there. ASIO's preferred recruits were trained investigators from military and police forces but, after that, it was a matter of who you knew. Dudley was a Mason and he knew a bloke in the Lodge who had been seconded to ASIO from the army. They used to go shooting together and this friend had suggested that Dudley would be good talent.

'Whaddya reckon?' Dudley asked. 'Should I take the secret job or go into the gun business?'

'A job with the government would be a good, settled life, with plenty of money,' said Joan, after the briefest of pauses. 'And it would be more reliable than gunsmithing.'

'All right. I'll take it,' he said. 'And they prefer married men, so we'd better get married.'

Joan put down the gun and gave her hand to Dudley.

10

Uneaten Cakes

Sydney, 26 November 1949

It wasn't much of a wedding.

They married in Sydney, so that Dudley's grandmother could come. The church, St Clement's Anglican Church at Mosman, was a grand Federation Gothic building with moulded brick, a slate roof and sandstone dressings. The minister was grand too. He was Rector Francis Hulme-Moir, who had been a famously roistering, story-telling, big-hearted wartime chaplain in the Middle East and the Pacific. He sang a hymn in a fine bass voice.

Twenty-year-old Joan looked lovely. She had saved up for an inexpensive biscuit-coloured dress with a U-shaped, lace-trimmed neckline. She was pencil slim and the dress fitted her perfectly.

Joan's dad had taught her to bake and she had spent the whole day before the wedding making magnificent cakes to eat after the ceremony. It wasn't until she walked down the aisle that she realised that almost no one had come to celebrate her wedding.

Dudley's grandmother had put her foot down. Amy Dean loved Dudley with a devouring love that permitted no others in his life. She had reared him, he was hers, and she refused him permission to marry. When he went ahead with his plans and invited her to the wedding, she said nothing. Right up to the day, he expected she would turn up, but not only did she shun the wedding, she told all of her children, including Dudley's mum Doris, that they were not allowed to go. The threats or bribes she used to keep them away are no longer known. Amy Dean wanted nothing to do with Joan.

There were stiff-necked people on both sides of the family. Joan's parents were travelling around Australia in a caravan at the time and also chose not to come to the wedding. Joan knew that her mother would have wanted to be there, and she kept hoping she would show up. But her father was angry at Joan for leaving home and for marrying, and he refused to come or to let his wife come.

Joan's beloved sister Clair was pregnant and living in Armidale, and she couldn't afford the petrol to travel to Sydney. By now Joan had lost track of her other sisters, Leah (named after her mother) and Bettina. They had married and gone their own ways. Somehow the close Ridgway family that had taken Dudley in so warmly had evaporated, driven apart by a terrible family secret that would not be acknowledged until years later.

So the only wedding guests were a Scottish woman—an old friend of Dudley's—and that woman's daughter. Even this was a supremely uncomfortable situation, because the friend's daughter had loved Dudley for a long time. She had hoped to marry him, and now she was one of the only people to witness his marriage to Joan.

'It's just as well I love him so much,' thought Joan sadly the next day, packing up cakes to give away to neighbours, 'because nobody else loves me.'

Both Joan and Dudley came from families where people disappeared. No wonder that Dudley was so good at disappearing and that Joan was so prepared to accept it.

11

Double Dealing

When Dudley proposed to Joan, they were very close, but there was a side to his life that he hadn't mentioned to her. Something he kept separate, for the time being at least.

During the war, the army was a melting pot. One of Dudley's corporals at Moorebank was a man called Abe Saffron, a man who would later become the nightclub and brothel owner known as 'The Boss of the Cross'. Dudley was a good boy who played in the Salvation Army Band, and Abe most definitely was not, but they became friends at Moorebank and their wartime friendship lasted for life. The wartime period was the only time that Abe worked for Dudley. Later on, the relationship was reversed.

Abe served in the army for less than four years (and, as Sue-Ellen commented later, goodness knows what he got up to, working in procurement!) before he left to set up Staccato, the first of his strip clubs in Kings Cross, offering a welcome service to the American GIs looking for fun in Sydney. He never wasted an opportunity and, while he was in the army, he spotted Dudley's talent for bookkeeping. Abe hired him to do the stocktakes for his clubs, a role Dudley continued to do for the rest of his life, even while he worked for ASIO. Dudley's books were the real ones, which were hidden, while somebody else prepared a different version for the taxation department. It would be interesting to know whether Dudley told ASIO about these extra-curricular activities, and how they viewed his work for Abe, but that is one of the many secrets Dudley took to his grave.

When Joan did find out about Abe, she always insisted that, whatever Abe was, Dudley wasn't a criminal—he just liked to stretch things to the limit. 'He was a rogue, but he was a good person,' she said. Into old age, Joan always saw Dudley as a larrikin, a wild boy, a joker, a great lover, a good and generous man, a loyal servant of his country. And her one true love.

These days we know of Abe Saffron as the Mr Big of Australian crime who had high-ranking members of the NSW police force, some judges and the premier of New South Wales, Sir Robert Askin, in his pocket. Like Al Capone, his only jail time was served for tax evasion, but his name has been linked with extortion, arson, prostitution, bribery, narcotics dealing and insurance fraud, as well as the disappearance of Juanita Nielsen, the thirty-eight-year-old heiress to the Mark Foy's department store fortune, in 1975.

But during Dudley's life, Abe Saffron liked to portray himself as a family man and a philanthropist and it is possible that Dudley did not know the extent of Abe's crimes. Joan knew from the beginning that Abe was Dudley's friend, but they did not discuss Abe's business life. By the time Abe had become notorious, Joan would have guessed, perhaps even known, that Abe's hospitality to Dudley included the use of the 'girls' in his brothels; she may have suspected that Dudley knew Abe's books were rigged. But she never believed Dudley knew about the possible murder, drugs and extortion. It probably took a long time for her to believe those things of their old friend, as she was highly sceptical of what she read in the newspapers.

Abe's wife Doreen was a country girl, like Joan, and she loved her charismatic husband and stuck by him despite his controlling habits (he wouldn't let her drive a car or use a chequebook), his public reputation as a sex addict and his twenty-year relationship with showgirl Rita Hagenfelds. Alan Saffron, their son, described his parents' marriage as abusive in his book *Gentle Satan*. He said he didn't think his mother was in denial about Abe, just dependent. He said that Abe 'wanted my mother and . . . would never let her go. Once my Dad owned something, it was never thrown out or discarded'.

Joan sometimes compared herself to Doreen, noting that her relationship with Dudley was better than Doreen's with Abe. This was setting a low benchmark for marital bliss.

Dudley looked up to Abe and it seems possible—likely, even—that Abe provided him with all the marriage guidance he ever got. The two marriages weren't the same. All the kids are still certain of Dudley's devotion to Joan. But both men were clear that work came first, which meant that they were away from home many nights and their wives could ask no questions. ASIO gave Dudley the perfect cover for that life; Abe told Doreen that he had a twenty-four-hour business that needed his guidance. Both wives swallowed their resentment, jealousy and grief, and continued to love their charming partners.

Mark was the only one of the Doherty children who had an opportunity to meet Abe in his business context. When he was sixteen, Mark went on holidays to Sydney with a school friend and his friend's family. Before he went, Dudley gave him a card for the Pink Pussycat club and said, 'Go and see Abe Saffron while you're in Sydney. He'll give you a good time.'

Mark and his friend discussed the offer but never took it up. 'Too chicken,' he grinned, when he told the story to his sisters later.

If the Doherty children had noticed anything odd about the Saffrons, they wouldn't have mentioned it. As Amanda said, 'We were disciplined not to ask questions. We were given the information we needed to know, and we just didn't ask.' The children loved their dad and accepted their mother's version of who he was.

Sue-Ellen remembers her dad as a good man, an Australian hero, a loving husband and father, and a faithful friend. And he was all those things. But he was good at keeping the different parts of his life in separate compartments. Joan was a trained observer and no fool, so she must have kept quiet about some of the things she suspected or knew. In an expression from her youth, she 'put up with things'. Secrecy and containment were features of their marriage from beginning to end.

They were also features of the newly formed ASIO. ASIO was set up primarily to prevent secret information from being leaked to the Soviet Union. Its mission was containment. Even within ASIO, nobody could know what anyone else was doing, in case one of those people was a mole, passing information to the communists.

Dudley's ability to keep things secret and separate was part of the selection criteria for working in ASIO. Who knows? Perhaps it was Dudley's skill at leading a double life that made his friend recommend him to ASIO as just the right type.

In November 1949, Dudley put on his new city suit and the shirt that Joan had carefully ironed and went to work at Agincourt, a four-storey building overlooking the Garden Island naval base on Sydney Harbour. It was the first headquarters for ASIO.

Deep in the basement of Agincourt was a giant Chubb safe sent out from London. It was so big that ASIO staff had to knock out the stonework from around the window to find a way to get it into the building. Inside were the Australian intercepts of the Venona files, the most closely guarded secret of the Cold War. Between 1940 and 1948, American crypta-nalysts had intercepted 3000 Soviet intelligence telegrams written in an 'unbreakable' code. Operation Venona was the code-breaking operation that unpicked the messages passing between the KGB in Moscow and its intelligence officers in embassies around the world.

The shocking discovery of Venona was that Moscow had highly placed spies inside the United States, British and Australian governments. The elaborate, intensive intelligence work taking place in the West to undermine the Soviet Union was in danger of being nullified completely by the Soviets' long-term placement of spies in government and the military.

The US and British governments were running deep, secret operations to neutralise and expose Soviet spies in their midst, but they saw Australia as being very casual in this regard. Ministers never locked their offices and in the 1940s Attorney-General H.V. 'Doc' Evatt was known to leave top-secret telegrams in his unlocked drawers for months at a time. In July 1948, Britain and the USA decided to exclude Australia from access to their signals intelligence until they were satisfied that Australia was serious about security. Anxious not to be left out of the intelligence club, prime minister Ben Chifley set up ASIO, known to its staff by a range of names including The Firm, The Company and The Business. Its primary task was to crack 'the case', the codename used to describe the deadly secret work of discovering which high-level Australians were spying for Moscow.

One of the Doherty children's strong memories of childhood is the way their parents followed international and local news with intense interest. That interest began in 1949, when Dudley began working for ASIO. From that time, international events took on new relevance to the young couple.

In 1948, the Soviet Union had undertaken determined military action to starve Berlin into submission and bring it under communist control, and the Western allies organised the Berlin airlift to carry supplies to the people of West Berlin. They flew more than 200,000 flights in one year, dropping 394,509 tons of fuel and food, until the USSR finally lifted the blockade in May 1949. The USSR had exploded its first atomic bomb just before Dudley joined ASIO and, early in 1950, the British-based German nuclear physicist Klaus Fuchs was sentenced to fourteen years in jail for passing British and American nuclear secrets to Soviet military intelligence. In October 1949—the month before Dudley joined ASIO—the Chinese communist leader Mao Zedong declared the creation of the People's Republic of China and, the following year, communist North Korea, with Soviet and Chinese backing, invaded South Korea.

So, although 'the case' and the Venona files were top secret, anyone reading the newspapers could see that communist organisations worldwide were pursuing global domination through espionage, sabotage and propaganda, as well as military action. ASIO's job was to resist with all its might. Working for ASIO was not just a day job: it was seen as saving the free world.

Joan firmly and finally put aside her dreams of becoming a doctor and adapted to her role as ASIO wife. ASIO at that time was a male-dominated business. In her memoir *More Cloak than Dagger*, former intelligence agent Molly Sasson describes her shock and dismay at finding deeply misogynistic attitudes in ASIO when she arrived to work in Australia in 1969 after a distinguished wartime career with British intelligence and a post-war career with MI5. She found much lower pay and dismal chances of promotion for women, and she received comments from supervisors about women belonging in the bedroom and the kitchen. These were the kinds of attitude you might expect in an organisation like ASIO, built up as it was from military and police old-boy networks. Before Molly's arrival, ASIO wives like Joan and female ASIO employees had taken male supremacy for granted.

Joan kept their home neat and was available at any hour of the day or night to cook meals for Dudley and other ASIO boys (as she called them) who might turn up hungry after long and irregular shifts. Her cooking became famous. But the family was supporting Dudley's grandmother, as well as paying the rent for a room in a house close to Dudley's work at Potts Point. Every penny was needed, so Joan took a typing job at chemical company ICI.

Joan was used to hard work. Work kept her mind off the loneliness of having a husband who could never talk to her about what he was doing and who often had to disappear for days at a time. She was happy, knowing she was with the man she loved and that they were building a better life for themselves. When she was afraid, Dudley would always encourage her. 'We'll be all right. You just wait and see,' he'd tell her.

One day, Dudley came home from work and told Joan she'd better stop working at ICI.

'Why?' asked Joan. 'I have to work.'

'You'd better come and work where I am,' said Dudley.

'Why?' asked Joan, thinking, *This conversation is like pulling teeth.*

'Because The Firm likes hiring married couples.'

It was a settled thing. Wives of ASIO officers were considered good candidates for employment as they were already bound to secrecy. Dudley arranged for Joan to go for an interview and to fill in a lot of forms and, by June 1950, they were both on the ASIO payroll.

On her first day at Agincourt, Joan was instructed to go behind 'the Green Door' to take up her new role. It was a daily disappearing act. The very existence of the room behind the shabby door was top secret.

One year earlier, Prime Minister Chifley had dropped in to see Giles Chippindall, Director-General of the Postmaster-General's Department. He told Chippindall he wanted ASIO to monitor certain telephones in Sydney. There would be no documents to support the prime minister's request. These were the very first ASIO telephone interceptions and, by the time Joan started work, fourteen phones belonging to suspects involved in 'the case' were being tapped.

At first, the intercepted conversations were taken down in longhand in Room 9 on the second floor of the Sydney office by ASIO investigators Dick Gamble, Les Scott and Ray Whitrod. By the time Joan arrived, the phone taps were taking place in the basement, in a room the size of a large cupboard, behind a green door. At that time, it was just an ordinary green door—the capital letters came later, when people understood what was happening behind it. Phone conversations were recorded on a Pyrox wire recorder. Joan worked behind that door, writing down intercepted phone conversations between people suspected of being Soviet spies, and recording their names and the times of the calls in a large logbook.

So, from day one, Joan spent her days working on the central project that had brought ASIO into existence and that was occupying its best minds. Very few ASIO officers at the time knew what was happening behind the Green Door. All the information Joan wrote out was attributed to a fictitious agent called Bob Kelly, so as not to give away the phone-bugging operation. Reports on the conversations she overheard would refer to 'our usual reliable source'. Joan had to figure out what was important or surprising in the conversations she transcribed and report them to somebody in charge.

One day Joan was interrupted at work by a knock at the door. When she opened it, a distinguished, military-looking gent said, 'Hello. Charlie Spry. I'd like to come in and talk to you.' It was the new director-general of ASIO, who had come to introduce himself.

'I can't let you in,' said Joan.

'You can let me in. I'm the DG.'

'Perhaps so. But you aren't on my list.'

Charles Spry was referred to as 'God'. Despite his short stature, he was the kind of person who caused people to jump to attention when he walked into a room. But he seemed to like Joan's attitude. He arranged with her supervisor, Ron Richards, to put himself on her list and, whenever he was in the building (he moved ASIO headquarters to Melbourne soon after, so wasn't always in Sydney), he would drop in to chat to her. Once Ron had reassured her that it was okay to speak to the director-general, she gave Charlie Spry a warm welcome and shared some of the things she had overheard from people on her list, including Australian Communist Party leader Lance Sharkey, and the man ASIO had identified as 'KLOD' in the Venona papers: Australian Communist Party organiser Walter Clayton.

She never spoke to Dudley about it, though. It was only in 2014, when she read *The Spy Catchers*, the first volume of the official history of ASIO, that Joan found out that Dudley had helped install the telephone-tapping equipment she was using. Both of them kept the details of their work strictly secret from each other.

Charles Spry was in charge of ASIO for the rest of the time Dudley and Joan worked there. His close relationship with prime minister Robert Menzies gave him the air, and possibly the reality, of being at the centre of all Australia's deepest and most secret decisions.

He was a hard-drinking man and, under his regime, ASIO had a drinking culture. He wanted ASIO to be a family, loyal to each other, personal and close, and he didn't go in for new-fangled ideas like training courses or computers—ASIO did not have any computers until the mid-seventies. He expected staff to work the way they would do during a war—without time clocks and unions and soft civilian working conditions.

Spry told his staff that their work was keeping democracy secure and that it entailed personal and domestic sacrifices. Joan and Dudley were proud to give their lives to the service of their country and they had total faith in their director-general. Working for ASIO was never 'just a job' for Joan. It was a solemn duty.

Joan worked twelve-hour shifts, concentrating furiously the whole time. The morning shift was staffed by another young woman, whose name was also Joan, and who became her friend. As they swapped shifts, they would take a few minutes to chat. Morning Joan would say, 'Oh, by the way, so-and-so's back in the picture.' Evening Joan would just say, 'Okay', but the mention of a name would be enough to alert her. They bantered with each other in scraps of Russian they had picked up, with *nyet* (no) and *nevazhno* (it doesn't matter) their favourite exclamations.

Many decades later, Joan said that she lost her political naivety during that time behind the Green Door. 'It was obvious from what I heard that people were doing bad things,' she told Sue-Ellen. 'I was a young person at that time, and I couldn't believe people would want to betray Australia like that.'

Joan and Dudley only saw each other in passing in those days. It was hard but Joan was glad to be doing interesting and useful work and to have money to put food on the table. In late 1950, they may have spent a little more time with each other when they began taking part in Operation Smile, ASIO's first bugging operation.

ASIO's work on 'the case' began with collecting information on Australians who were passing information to Russia, but agents soon began looking at Russians based in Australia as well. Fedor Nosov, who represented Soviet news agency TASS in Australia, was thought to be the person under the cover name of 'TEKHNIK' in the Venona material. By mid-1949, ASIO was opening Nosov's mail, tapping his phone and occasionally following him. Nosov lived in an apartment in Darlinghurst, in a building on Kings Cross Road called Kaindi.

To set the stage for Operation Smile, ASIO rented the apartment above Nosov's, and Dudley and Joan moved in. Ray

Whitrod (who later became Queensland's police commissioner) was part of their moving-in committee. Under Ray's supervision, an MI5 officer bored holes through from the Dohertys' flat into the ceiling of Nosov's flat, around the central light fitting, and installed a microphone. Wires ran from that to a reel-to-reel tape recorder in the living room of the Doherty flat. When Whitrod peered through the hole in the floor to check the result, he noticed that not only was the microphone clearly visible from the room below but that they had dropped plaster on the floor. He sped downstairs and persuaded the caretaker to let him into Nosov's flat to clean it up.

Joan's job was still to listen and transcribe, but now she was listening through large headphones to live conversations in the room directly below, rather than to phone conversations. Dudley was still away working long hours, but at least Joan was home when he returned. Although she was not usually alone. Typically a director was also in the room, listening in to conversations on a separate set of headphones.

ASIO recruited Bill Marshall, a Belarussian émigré, to translate the tapes of Nosov's conversations when they were in Russian. Joan remembers that Bill would arrive at the apartment at 10 p.m., and she could ask him questions about any foreign words she had heard and discuss any suspicions she had about the conversations she had transcribed. With Bill's help, she found she had a talent for picking up foreign languages. Occasionally she had to transcribe a whole conversation in Russian, Polish or Serbian, and she was surprised at how much she could understand. Joan's father had been good with languages. He was reputed to speak seven languages. Later on,

Amanda discovered that she had inherited the gift for languages too. She could understand the uncomplimentary things her mother-in-law said about her in Greek, thinking she would not understand.

Despite the crowded conditions in their new home, the Dohertys had enough time together for Joan to fall pregnant. Mark Doherty was born in the apartment at Kaindi in 1951, and this placid baby became an unwitting player in ASIO's first covert bugging operation. Joan continued with the listening work where possible, letting Mark sleep in the room furthest from the living room, but she was supported by a male ASIO operative. If she needed to take Mark out for a walk or go shopping, ASIO had the job covered. When she went out with Mark, Dudley would often suggest she make the acquaintance of people who lived in the neighbourhood so she could find out who they were. This was Joan's introduction to the principle that anyone at all could be a 'person of interest' and that it was always worth meeting people and observing them. In the process, she also made some friends—in particular, she enjoyed the company of a couple called Patsy and James who lived in the same building. James liked to dress up in women's clothing and go out at night; perhaps he asked the elegant Joan for help with planning his outfits.

It was exciting work, but it was also frustrating, because Joan only heard scraps of information that didn't tell her the whole story. She remembers transcribing many of Nosov's conversations with unionists, especially with members of the Building Workers' Industrial Union. She heard that some union leaders believed unions had a dual purpose—not only to improve pay and conditions for workers but to educate them in Moscow-style radical politics.

One of the regular visitors to the Dohertys' flat was a colourful ASIO informer called Dr Michael Bialoguski—a medical practitioner and a violinist who had escaped from the Soviet Union in 1941 and had come to Australia using forged papers. Later on, he would play a significant role in the Petrov Affair, helping to confirm ASIO's suspicions that Soviet Embassy staff Vladimir and Evdokia Petrov were spies for the KGB—the Soviet intelligence service. At this stage, however, he was just another informer, getting five pounds a week from ASIO for information about Russian immigrants, while also running an abortion clinic. Joan disliked Bialoguski intensely; she never trusted him and called him 'a two-timer'. She was entitled to her own views as long as she recorded only the facts.

One day Nosov came up to the flat and banged on the door. Joan opened it but refused to let him in. 'My baby is sleeping,' she said, holding firmly on to the door he was pushing. 'You are spying on me. I know,' he shouted at her. 'Nonsense,' she said. 'You are imagining things.' Nosov called the owner of the building, who Joan remembers as a wealthy man from Papua New Guinea. 'Ah, you're just imagining things,' he soothed Nosov. 'It's just a little family.' Eventually Nosov went away and they continued their work.

Sue-Ellen was born in 1953, fifteen months after Mark. She was a live wire from the beginning, who didn't waste much time on sleeping, and Joan decided she couldn't look after two children and ASIO. She resigned from her ASIO duties and dropped off the payroll. 'After that, I only worked for ASIO nineteen hours a day,' she later joked, poker faced.

It wasn't that much of a joke. Resignation simply meant that Joan took her orders from Dudley instead of from another supervisor. Dudley quickly worked out that a woman with young children was a perfect cover for a spy. In particular, he used Joan and the children, as often as possible, to sit in public places and listen to conversations. From 1953 to 1970, Joan continued to work for ASIO, without pay. She may have made ironic remarks about her situation, but she never seriously questioned her patriotic duty. She couldn't be certain whether ASIO officially sanctioned her work, or whether she was just helping Dudley on the quiet—it wasn't a need-to-know issue.

In May 1954, at the Royal Commission on Espionage, senior counsel, Victor Windeyer, blew the cover of NSW journalist and undercover ASIO agent Mercia Masson, in an attempt to expose subversive activity by the man she was watching, communist journalist Rex Chiplin. Masson spoke later of the pain of giving evidence against Chiplin and others who had become her close friends, even though she had disagreed with their politics. After her identity was exposed, they were no longer her friends, she lost her job, and she believed that her life and that of her child were put at risk.

Joan remembers being assigned, at the time of the Royal Commission, to listen to one of Masson's private conversations in a cafe. Even though she was an agent, Masson was probably not suspicious of the pretty young mother with her babies sitting on the other end of the bench seat, writing busily in her journal. Joan did not know at the time whose conversation she was listening to, nor did she understand the way Masson's life was being destroyed by her exposure during the Royal Commission.

Like all other ASIO operatives, Joan had been given her own instructions, but she'd never had any idea how they fitted into the bigger picture, or even if there was a bigger picture. She wondered sometimes if the work she did for ASIO was really necessary—was it any use? And she couldn't talk to anyone about it, not even Dudley. It felt like a dream, sometimes. But then she would see or hear something quite definite, something that assured her she was part of a team tracking down dangerous spies, and her determination would be renewed.

12

The Petrovs

Brisbane, 1956

Joan was on her knees beside the tub, bathing Sue-Ellen and
Mark, when she met Russian defector Evdokia Petrov. Dudley
ushered Mrs Petrov into the room and, while the children
squealed and splashed, the two women made stilted conversation. Mrs Petrov had come to look Joan over and decide whether
she and her husband Vladimir would come to live with the
Doherty family for two months.

It was November 1956 and the Olympic Games were about
to be held in Melbourne. There was enormous excitement in
sport-mad Australia: it was the first time an Olympic Games
had been held in the Southern Hemisphere—or even outside
Europe and North America—and the Duke of Edinburgh was
going to open the Games. Television broadcasting was starting
up for the first time, to record the event.

But the Olympics are never just about sport. Joan and Dudley, inveterate news followers, had been closely following the political lead-up to the 'friendly games', in which sporting venues turned into battlefields, with the Soviet Union and the USA fighting for supremacy. The Netherlands, Spain and Switzerland withdrew from the Games in protest at the Soviet Union's presence. The Soviet Union had recently crushed an attempted revolution in Hungary and those two bitter adversaries met in a furious and bloody semi-final of the water polo contest. A total of forty-six athletes defected from the East to the West during the Games.

Colonel Vladimir Petrov and his wife, Captain Evdokia Petrov, had arrived in Australia in 1951 on the ocean liner *SS Orcades*. He was the third secretary at the Soviet Embassy in Canberra and she was a code clerk, but their real role was intelligence; they were notable for having survived a series of bloodthirsty purges during the twenty years of their intelligence careers in Moscow.

One of Petrov's roles in Australia was to recruit people to penetrate the organisations of anti-Soviet Russians and Balts. He met, and cultivated, the young Polish doctor, Michael Bialoguski, who had many patients from the Soviet Union and was open about his pro-Soviet views. Petrov gave him the code name Grigorii. What he didn't realise was that Bialoguski was already working as an undercover agent for ASIO. The two became constant companions, drinking together at the California Cafe and Abe Saffron's Roosevelt Club during Petrov's regular visits to Sydney, and cruising Kings Cross in the early mornings looking for women. Joan heard all about their adventures as she listened to conversations in the Nosov apartment—no doubt inspiring her dislike and distrust of Bialoguski.

Bialoguski suggested to ASIO that Petrov might be a candidate for defection and, with ASIO's permission, he courted Petrov: first with hints about the pleasures of life in Australia, and finally with a direct offer to buy the Petrovs a chicken farm outside Sydney with the unlikely name of Dream Acres.

Moscow's MVD (the Soviet Ministry of Internal Affairs) realised fairly quickly that Petrov was not producing results from his intelligence work and was drawing negative attention to the Soviet Embassy with a series of drunken incidents, including one in which he nearly ran over a police constable. Evdokia was considered rude and indiscreet by other embassy staff. She made disparaging comments about the dowdy Moscow women she worked with and claimed that the Soviet ambassador, Nikolai Lifanov, was causing troubles for her and Vladimir because she had refused the ambassador's sexual advances.

In January 1954, Petrov was threatened with recall to Moscow and he knew enough about Moscow politics to believe he would be executed on his return. He shared his feelings with Bialoguski and, shortly afterwards, ASIO briefed Prime Minister Menzies on the possibility of a defection.

On 3 April 1954, ASIO agent Ron Richards drove Vladimir Petrov to a safe house on Sydney's north shore and handed him a parcel containing £5000. In exchange, Petrov passed Richards the documents in his satchel. Petrov had now defected—but his wife didn't know yet.

When the Soviets discovered that Petrov had defected, they imprisoned Evdokia in a single room of the embassy and booked her on a BOAC flight from Sydney to Moscow on 19 April.

The time of the flight was publicised, and a crowd of intensely emotional people—mostly refugees from the Soviet Union—came to witness Evdokia's departure. The crowd watched her apparently being frogmarched to the plane by two grim Soviet apparatchiks. They called out to her, believing she was being dragged to her death. They saw her lose a shoe as they pushed towards the plane and heard her cry out in fear.

The dramatic photos in the paper next day prompted urgent national action. Prime Minister Menzies instructed Charles Spry to approach Evdokia at the airport in Darwin and ask if she wanted to seek asylum in Australia. After being asked several times, and arranging to speak to her husband by phone, she agreed to put herself under the protection of the Australian Government.

These events had occurred two years before Evdokia appeared in Joan's bathroom. The Petrovs were by then living in Melbourne and, as the Olympics drew closer, they were desperately afraid. Nobody knew better than they did how easy it would be for Russian intelligence officers to come to Australia with the Olympic team, posing as coaches or physiotherapists: it would take only one of them to assassinate the Petrovs. ASIO decided to move the Petrovs out of Melbourne to safety for two months.

Petrov followers called it 'the lost two months'. Nobody knew what happened to the Petrovs during that time until ASIO historians tracked down Joan in Brisbane in 2011 and briefly recorded that they had been staying with the Doherty family. No other details of those two months have been recorded until now.

At first, the Petrovs were sent to stay with the family of ASIO agent Leo Carter outside Sydney, but Evdokia was not happy there. She told Joan afterwards that Mrs Carter did not wash vegetables before she peeled them, and Evdokia did not think that was hygienic. She expected both the washing and the peeling of vegetables, and she wanted to stay somewhere else.

ASIO's personnel officer, who Joan remembers was called 'Mac', asked Dudley whether he and Joan would be prepared to look after the Petrovs. Dudley had been transferred to Brisbane earlier that year and Mac suggested that a young family in Queensland would be a good cover for the Russian defectors. They would look like a family group, with grandparents. Dudley agreed; the next step was for Evdokia to inspect the Doherty household and decide whether it was acceptable to her.

The meeting of the two women—the Russian spy and the Australian spy—in a cramped Brisbane bathroom was not a great social success. Evdokia told ASIO she thought Joan was rather a dull, housewifely sort of woman. But she thought she had probably run out of choices in the strange, primitive country she had found herself in. She agreed to go and live with the Dohertys.

ASIO arranged for them all to stay in a two-storey house in the centre of the booming holiday town of Surfers Paradise south of Brisbane. Sue-Ellen, who was three at the time, can remember the lush yellow flowers of the allamanda plant that grew out the front of the white house.

In the fifties, Surfers Paradise was known as Queensland's playground, with golden beaches and all-year-round sunshine. In the state's capital, ninety minutes to the north, prim Brisbanites went out to dinner on special occasions at Italian restaurants with white tablecloths. Gold Coast people ate under umbrellas in outdoor cafes. You could walk right through town in your bathers without anyone noticing. It was a family place, where children and dogs were part of the fun anywhere you went, including the beach parties with rock 'n' roll dancing and singing, and riotous trips on overcrowded pleasure boats. Dinner usually meant barbecues with overcooked steak and eggs, or prawns and beer, followed by fruit salad with mango, pawpaw and pineapple grown in the rich soil of the hinterland.

The Petrovs lived upstairs in the allamanda-covered house and the Dohertys lived downstairs—the usual living arrangement for ASIO agents sheltering people. The only instructions ASIO gave the Dohertys were 'Keep 'em out of trouble' and 'Watch Jack'. Jack was the cover name for Vladimir Petrov, and they soon found out why they had to watch him. Jack was often drunk, bad-tempered and unreliable.

'He was a peasant from Siberia,' said Joan, dismissively. She was talking to Sue-Ellen, years later, when Sue-Ellen was on her quest to find out more about her childhood. 'None of us liked him. He was strange, very crude. He always knew better than everyone else. You were wrong or bloody wrong.'

Evdokia was different. After a stiff beginning, Joan and Evdokia quickly became great friends—as much as it's possible for an ASIO spy and a reluctant Soviet defector to be friends. The Dohertys called Evdokia 'Peewee', for reasons that no one can remember now, and they found her to be an intelligent and caring person. Later Peewee confessed to Joan that she had told ASIO she thought Joan would be boring, but she had changed her mind. She decided Joan was great fun to be with.

Peewee was fifteen years older than twenty-six-year-old Joan, but they were both attractive women. Peewee liked to flirt with men and to talk about clothes. Neither woman had much money for dresses, but they loved to window-shop together in the new boutiques that were opening up in Surfers. Peewee was always beautifully dressed, unlike her husband, who wore a uniform of grubby old khaki shorts and socks with sandals. Neither of them wore disguises; they just dressed to fit in as part of an Australian family group.

Peewee would tell Joan why she liked a certain outfit but might say, 'It's not for you with your long legs. You're different.' One day she helped Joan choose a reversible Paula Stafford bikini, a daring thing to wear on the Gold Coast in the fifties. Four years earlier, model Ann Ferguson had been expelled from a beach in Surfers Paradise because her Paula Stafford bikini was too revealing.

Their days quickly fell into what looked like a comfortable holiday pattern. Dudley would take Jack and five-year-old Mark out to the river to fish. 'Good. He's gone,' Peewee would say to Joan, glad to be rid of her husband. 'We can enjoy ourselves.' Joan and Peewee would take Sue-Ellen to the pub on the corner of Cavill Avenue and sit in the beer garden. Sue-Ellen would play on the swings, and Joan and Peewee would sip their drinks and watch the young people.

'We both liked watching people,' said Joan. 'We had a lot in common.' Indeed they had, as both were trained watchers. But they did not talk shop. Not ever. They were just two pretty women having a drink.

Peewee didn't like swimming, but she loved to walk with Joan on the beach. There was a small rock pool that Sue-Ellen could play in, and Joan and Peewee would lie on the sand beside her and play Chinese chequers. Sue-Ellen was fascinated to see her mother and Peewee playing a game with marbles.

Peewee loved Sue-Ellen. She took her everywhere with her and paid special attention to her small feet. She was always asking Sue-Ellen whether her feet hurt and making sure she wore comfortable shoes. She took her out and bought her 'correct' shoes, kneeling on the floor to check there was enough room around the child's little toes.

Peewee's only child—Irina, a daughter from her first marriage—had died of meningitis in the Soviet Union at the age of two. Peewee talked about her little girl to Joan, while she held Sue-Ellen and played with her. She had loved Irina's father, but he had been arrested by the Soviets soon after Irina's birth and taken away forever. When Irina died suddenly and shockingly, it was Vladimir Petrov who comforted her; she thought he was a kind and devoted man, and she married him. By the time she was living with the Dohertys, she no longer thought he was a kindly man. When she discussed him with Joan, she would say, 'He's just a . . .' and make a rude spitting noise.

The unspoken rule was that the Dohertys would not visit the Petrovs upstairs without an invitation, as that would be an invasion of privacy, but the Petrovs could always visit the

Dohertys. Sue-Ellen would have ignored the rule and followed Peewee upstairs if she were allowed, but Joan forbade it and Peewee would shoo her out. Sue-Ellen would cry but Joan was firm.

There was more than protocol at stake: Joan was determined not to let Sue-Ellen see what she herself had seen upstairs. 'Petrov would sit on a big rattan chair and he'd take his trousers off and just sit there all exposed,' said Joan. 'You'd say now he was a dirty old man.' Joan's tone as she said this was objective, non-committal, but that was her professional spy voice. The nightmares she endured then were not about Russian assassins but about the presence of grubby Petrov and his penis in her home, near her children. She watched Sue-Ellen like a hawk, knowing only too well what some men would do to small children.

Peewee was open about her disgust for her husband's exhibitionism, though she didn't seem to have been afraid of him. 'Put your pecker in your pants,' she would snap at him. And when he didn't, she would bite his penis, to annoy him. And laugh about it afterwards with Joan. For her, he just seemed to be a big, gross blob, perpetually under her feet. She rolled her eyes at him, spat out his name and made scathing remarks about his body without ever seeming to fear reprisal.

On rainy days they all stayed inside, and Peewee would come to Joan's part of the house. Peewee didn't cook. Her idea of preparing a meal was to take a thick wedge of bread and spread jam and sour cream on it. That was her favourite thing to eat. But Joan was an accomplished cook and Peewee loved to watch her prepare food. She often made special dishes for Peewee: beef stroganoff and borscht, things that would give her back a sense of home.

Peewee was grievously homesick. She believed she had been forced to stay in Australia. In those long afternoons in Joan's kitchen, she told Joan her side of the story about the defection. She said that her husband was a weak and cowardly man and she blamed him bitterly for defecting in secret, without telling her. After he made his secret deal with ASIO, Peewee had been put under house arrest in the Soviet embassy in Canberra and then was told she would be escorted back to the Soviet Union by KGB couriers. Peewee had no idea her husband had defected and believed that ASIO had kidnapped him. When the crowd mobbed her at Sydney airport, she cried out in fear of them, not of her guards. She told Joan how, when her plane touched down in Darwin, ASIO officials wrestled with her guards, disarmed them and offered her a chance to defect. They gave her a chance to talk by phone to her husband and, when she realised he had defected, she knew that she would be assassinated if she went home.

The agonising decision she had to make at the airport in Darwin was to go home to certain death, or to defect, knowing that her mother and her beloved sister Tamara might be arrested or killed. Tamara had a heart condition and Peewee was afraid she would no longer be allowed her medicines or that she would not have a place to live. She chose to stay, but years later she still grieved, crying, wailing, keening among the vegetables in Joan's hospitable kitchen.

She hated her husband, but he was the only person she could speak with in her first language. He was the only person who knew her family and the places she loved and the skills she had. He was repulsive to her, but they understood each other. All this she spoke of to Joan on those long rainy afternoons in the kitchen, while Sue-Ellen played close by.

When she was calmer, she would ask Joan questions about Australian food and culture. She was interested in knowing how the education system worked and explained to Joan that, in the Soviet Union, you were not allowed to go straight to university from school. You had to work for a year first. Both women, the communist and the dyed-in-the-wool Liberal, agreed that was a better system.

She asked about sexual practices in Australia too. At what age did young people have sex? There was nothing they couldn't talk about in that intimate space—except work.

They kept the front door locked all the time they talked and there was a little place behind the curtains at the front of the house where Joan or Peewee would stand sometimes to check if anyone was outside. If there was someone walking in the yard, or if someone stood still on the footpath, they would watch in silence until the person moved on. Both of them knew the signs of danger, but they were experienced watchers, and they kept quiet about their fears and carried on as usual.

⌒

While the women chatted and watched and waited, Dudley took 'Jack' fishing in the river, in a small boat with Mark. Mark was a quiet boy, and he didn't disturb them; these days he can't remember what the men spoke about. Jack was a country boy—he had started his career as an apprentice blacksmith in

Siberia—and Dudley loved the Australian bush. Perhaps they talked about farming as well as fishing. And both of them had made or mended guns when they were young, so they may have chatted about guns and ammunition. Or perhaps they were silent, as fishermen often are. Jack's English was not as good as Peewee's and it was a strain for him to speak in English for too long.

In the evenings, Jack and Peewee could be together upstairs, but Peewee often slipped down to join the Dohertys for dinner while Jack went to the pub. She didn't like being at home when he came back drunk and she felt comfortable with Dudley, Joan and the children.

Surfers Paradise was seen as a raunchy, happening sort of place at the time. There was a new local fashion of people going to the pub in their pyjamas and people were both more casual and more exotic than in Brisbane. But it was still a small town and it is interesting to wonder what the locals would have made of this gruff Soviet, drinking heavily and talking loudly in a mix of Russian and English—especially as his face had been in the newspapers regularly over the previous few years, and Cold War fears were still alive.

One night Jack was very drunk and got lost on his way home from the pub. He knocked on the door of somebody else's house, then panicked and told them who he was. The neighbours told him how to get back to the house, but they rang a newspaper as soon as he'd left. Jack does not seem to have been a very good spy. Joan was certain then that it was his wife who had the brains, and who was the real catch for ASIO.

Dudley got a phone call from another agent who tipped him off that the press was on their trail. The agent told him to go to a safe house in Redcliffe, a bayside holiday town just north of Brisbane city, but to lose the press who would be following in a car.

Both families had been living out of their suitcases. Sue-Ellen still lives out of her suitcase when she goes on holidays—she grew up thinking that's what you did. They quickly heaved their luggage into the two ASIO FJ Holdens, and divided the families into two groups, making sure the Petrovs were separated. Joan didn't drive at that time, so there must have been another ASIO agent there to drive the second car. Having ASIO agents around, even on holidays, was nothing special.

The distance from Surfers Paradise to Redcliffe is 110 kilometres, and normally it would take two hours of careful driving to get there. The Dohertys took a day to make the trip, driving slowly in long circles, ambling like sightseers. The two drivers kept their eyes on the rear-vision mirrors, making sure they weren't being tailed. They were packed into hot cars in glaring sunlight for the interminable drive, and the tension was palpable. The Petrovs were sure that any publicity identifying their whereabouts would be fatal. They never trusted the Australian Government to keep them safe from deadly Soviet intelligence assassins—agents that the Petrovs themselves had helped to train and operate. Jack, in the car with Dudley, was gruff and bad-tempered but everyone else, even the children, knew how to keep things calm. Joan had packed delicious homemade biscuits and sandwiches, and she and Peewee played

I Spy with the children, and sang songs and talked nonsense with Sue-Ellen.

Finally, Dudley signalled to Joan that they were clear and both cars arrived separately at two new flats that were being built on the water at Redcliffe. The flats were almost ready for people to move in to, and ASIO had arranged to occupy them. As before, the Petrovs took the top flat and the Dohertys moved in below. The children remember the round windows at the front, like portholes. Released from the car at last, they ran up and down the stairs excitedly.

They prepared to settle down to their normal holiday pursuits, but Dudley had been tipped off that the KGB was in the area and looking for the Petrovs. He took Jack and Mark out fishing as a way of hiding during the day. Sue-Ellen wanted to go too, and she started to cry when Dudley said she couldn't. Peewee soothed her. 'Come on, darlink, we will do somesink,' she promised. And she sat down with Sue-Ellen and painted her toenails. Sue-Ellen was so excited that she forgot all about wanting to go fishing. Meanwhile Mark remembers sitting in a boat quietly under the bridge that crossed Bramble Bay, fishing, or at least pretending to fish. They waited there most of the day until Dudley decided the coast was clear.

This time their hideout only lasted for a couple of days. The newsagent was a couple of doors away from their flats, and he recognised Jack. There was a knock at the door, which they didn't answer. Dudley was on the phone straightaway. After the call, he turned around and said, 'We're not going to stay here.'

They loaded up the cars again and travelled north, in a complicated series of loops and double-backs, to the Sunshine Coast. Dudley told the children to get on the floor of the car while they drove. After a little while, Mark whispered, 'Hang on, there's a basket down here.' Joan always had a picnic handy, in case they were caught outside for any length of time. As an adult, Mark has forgotten everything the Petrovs ever said, but he has never forgotten his discovery of the basket with the delicious marshmallow biscuits on wheatmeal, with hundreds and thousands on top. Joan didn't miss much, and she probably knew exactly why the children were so quiet for the rest of the trip. But in their memories, it was a delightful and wicked secret to be hiding on the ground, munching on marshmallow biscuits until they arrived at their new holiday house on the lake at Moffat Beach, Caloundra.

They remained on high alert but there were no further incidents, although there was a false alarm when a woman came asking for directions and caused a flutter of fear in the household. The only real danger occurred when Mark walked into the lake to see how far he could go, and Sue-Ellen followed him in and had to be rescued. Looking after Sue-Ellen, keeping Jack out of the pub, avoiding the media and dodging KGB agents kept Joan and Dudley fully occupied on their beach holiday.

Nerve-racking as the whole experience was, Joan remembers it fondly because of the friendship she formed with Peewee. It was rare for her to be intimate with another woman—she had too many secrets to keep. Although she and Evdokia Petrov had been trained to deceive and defeat each other's intelligence agencies, they understood each other very well and there was no need for deception with each other. Joan could be more fully herself with the Russian agent than she could with any Australians.

After the Olympic Games were over, ASIO whisked the Petrovs away to the Melbourne suburb of Bentleigh, where they lived under the assumed names of Sven and Maria Anna Allyson. He worked as a storeman and she as a clerk. Before she left, Peewee took Joan's hand and whispered, 'You are a very special person.'

The Petrovs, who had survived poverty, bitter Russian winters and Stalinist purges, lived quietly together until Jack died in 1991. We can only imagine the discontent in that unloving household. Peewee was finally reunited with her beloved sister, who survived and came to Australia to settle near her, and died eleven years after her husband.

Joan often wondered about Peewee, but she was not allowed to contact her. It wasn't until many years later that she discovered that Dudley's colleague, Sue-Ellen's 'Uncle Mick', had been assigned to watch over the Petrovs in their home in Melbourne. She never knew whether her friend was alive or not until she read of Evdokia's death in the newspaper.

Sue-Ellen was with her mother when Joan read Evdokia's obituary on 19 July 2002. 'Why are you so sad, Mum?' she asked. Sue-Ellen was always the one who wanted to know why.

Joan answered quietly, 'Peewee has died. She was my friend.'

13

Joan Works Undercover

Peewee Petrov may have been the last intimate friend Joan ever had. After Dudley's transfer to Brisbane in 1956, Joan no longer enjoyed the easy camaraderie she had shared with 'Morning Joan' behind the Green Door. Far from the bustle of Kings Cross, she was in a new town, working undercover in that loneliest of 1950s careers: suburban housewife.

The family lived for a few months with Dudley's mum in Milton. Doris gave them a warm welcome, and they loved her, but there wasn't room for an extra family in her tiny cottage. So Joan found a post-war wooden cottage on Crown Street, Bardon, an inner Brisbane suburb. They bought it and lived there for six years, except for a few weeks in a boarding house, until their house on Kilmaine Street in The Gap was built.

In Brisbane, for fourteen years, Joan kept house and raised her children while Dudley went out to work—just like all the other housewives. Except that Joan was training her kids in espionage and keeping a careful watch on her neighbours. Russian agents might exist, even in The Gap, a leafy, middle-class suburb.

She was a member of the school P&C committee and she watched people there. Left-wing people such as unionists were automatically objects of suspicion, especially if they were active in the P&C too. But she didn't ignore people with right-wing views either. Sometimes someone would say something strange that didn't fit with the rest of a conversation. That would raise flags for Joan and, the next time she was at a committee meeting, she would make a point of sitting next to them. Joan had a pleasant, attentive way of speaking with people that quickly put them at ease. She would chat, or she would just listen without appearing to do so. Sometimes someone would mention a name that Joan had heard behind the Green Door.

'These people all interlink, you know,' she explained to me later. 'Most people miss what is going on in front of them. They just see the surface of things. They don't watch and see that something is not right with a person, like the wrong piece of a puzzle.'

Sometimes she would put in a report to ASIO about something she had seen or heard. She never knew what happened to her reports, or whether the people she named were found to be spies.

Dudley worked hard. He would disappear for days—even weeks—at a time. Fear was a normal state for Joan in those days. When Dudley was away, she never knew what he was doing, whether he was safe or when he would come home. She worried about her children whenever they were out of sight.

She knew firsthand the reality of the KGB. She worried if a stranger walked down the street, or a new neighbour moved in. When you worked for ASIO, you had to be aware and cautious every moment. It was no good panicking; you had to be hyper-alert all the time. Joan was not on the ASIO payroll anymore, but it is not a job you walk away from when you resign. She still saw herself as under oath. Sue-Ellen remembers her mother as being too thin in those years, never more than a size 8, and always on edge.

Apart from watching for enemy agents, Joan had all the other worries of a woman alone. She had to deal with house hunting and plumbing problems and issues with the neighbours. She used to pick up two little girls from school for a neighbour and she would keep the girls at her place until her neighbour came home from work. The kids got on well with her kids, so it was a good arrangement. One night, the kids' father came to pick up the girls, instead of their mother. He saw the black negligees on the clothesline; Dudley had bought them for Joan from a little French shop. The man wanted to come into the house. Joan said she'd bring the girls out, but the father said, 'Don't bring 'em out now. Put on one of those black nighties and come out.' Always resourceful, Joan rang a friend of Dudley's who lived nearby, and he came and moved the neighbour on.

It was after they moved to Brisbane that Joan found out about Dudley's women. She was observant, but his interest in her never waned. He called her his 'JoJo'; he brought her gifts of chocolates and flowers and silk lingerie. He couldn't keep his hands off her. He adored her. He was her great lover and protector, the one who always encouraged her and kept her going when she fell into her dark moods. She says so even today, and all the children remember it.

And yet he was away so often. And there were the prostitutes he visited with oysters, and the girls at Abe's clubs. He said he was working. She kept asking if he was sleeping with other women and he finally admitted it. He was relieved to be able to talk about it with her and it didn't change anything he did. He said it was separate, it was work, it didn't have anything to do with them and their undying love.

Joan thought about leaving, but what would become of her and the children? In those days, there was no supporting parent's pension. Her parents wouldn't help her. She was alone, with no one to advise her. She would wait. What else could she do?

She was patient and she was strong. She was a perfect ASIO wife, supporting Dudley in every way. The only sign she sometimes gave of her pent-up feelings was the silent treatment she gave Dudley. Sometimes he could not get her to speak for hours or days. It confused him. He used to ask the kids what he had done wrong. But Joan knew that if she spoke, she might say things that could never be taken back. So she simply took away the warmth of her regard and let him shiver. She kept her feelings and her words strictly contained.

In 1957 Joan had news from her sister Clair. Their father had died. He had been running down a set of steps while exiting a building. He never walked anywhere. He was a vigorous man, always in a hurry. But somehow he had fallen, maybe his heart had given out, and he never got up again.

Joan did not go to his funeral. 'How would I get the time, with my busy life?' she said. But there was something else.

Joan, aged 12, with her mother, Leah Ridgway, in their city clothes for a daytrip to Sydney. They were snapped by a street photographer and took the photo home to mark this special occasion.

Harry Ridgway would not have known his daughters were wearing two-piece swimsuits on this visit to Bondi Beach—he definitely wouldn't have approved. Enjoying this illicit adventure are (*left to right*): Joan, Clair, a friend, and Bettina. Joan is 13.

The Ridgway family go to town. They are (*left to right*): Joan, Clair, Leah (the daughter), Harry, Leah (the mother), Bettina.

Dudley, aged 5, at his grandmother's house in Glebe, where he lived while his mother worked in western New South Wales as a station cook.

Dudley proudly shows off the euphonium he played in the Salvation Army band. After the tram accident that took his leg, he received help and encouragement from Brigadier Johns of the Sydney Salvos. Dudley was a loyal member of the Salvos all his life.

Corporal Dudley Doherty, soon after he joined the Supply team in the 5th Base Ordnance Depot at Moorebank, NSW. This photo was taken around the time he first met Joan.

Dudley and Joan on a night out in Sydney in the early 1950s when they were both working for ASIO.

A Sydney street photo of Dudley and Joan during their courting days. Joan has her angry look—possibly because Dudley arrived late. She had to get used to that, and to not knowing where he was much of the time.

Dudley in his ASIO suit in Sydney. The children recognise this as his yellow tie—the flashiest one he had. He soon learned not to wear it. 'My job is not to be seen,' he told the kids when they suggested he wear more colourful ties.

Agincourt, ASIO's first headquarters, at 12 Wylde Street, Potts Point, on Sydney Harbour, was a place of legend for the Doherty children: a secret building where heroic men and women (mostly men) worked tirelessly to keep Australia safe. Sue-Ellen finally visited it after her father's death. (ASIO)

The Kaindi apartment building at King's Cross Road, Darlinghurst, was the site of ASIO's first covert bugging operation. The target was TASS journalist Fedor Nosov, and the faint line in the upper right of the photograph points to his apartment. Mark and Sue-Ellen Doherty were born in the apartment directly above. (ASIO)

The Doherty family lived in this house on Crown Street in Brisbane for seven years, after moving there in 1956. It was a typical house of the times, with chooks in the backyard and a flourishing mango tree.

Sue-Ellen and Mark at a farm in Brookfield, on the outskirts of Brisbane, which they often visited. The farm was owned by an ASIO agent, a good friend of the Dohertys, and the children learned to ride ponies there.

Sue-Ellen showing off her dance moves to her dad on the verandah at Crown Street.

The Dohertys at a typical weekend picnic in Brisbane with friends. It is one of the few photos showing Dudley's wooden leg. The ASIO car—always a Holden—is in the background.

Dudley with Mark, Sue-Ellen and Amanda in the brand-new house at Kilmaine Street, The Gap. They moved in on 22 November 1963, the day US President John F. Kennedy was assassinated. All ASIO agents were called in to work that day, so Joan had to move house on her own.

A rare picture of Dudley Doherty at work. He was at a Chinese function with one of the many families he befriended (and used in his information-gathering activities).

Arthur Goldstein, from the USA, one of the visitors Dudley brought home from the ships—handsome and charming, he brought whole cartons of Hershey bars. Here he drinks a beer that Dudley must have bought specially for him—the Dohertys usually didn't have any alcohol in the house.

This defining photograph of Dudley's friend Abe Saffron was taken at his Roosevelt nightclub in January 1951. The Doherty children noticed their Dad was always very tired when he came home from doing the books for Abe. (*The Sydney Morning Herald*)

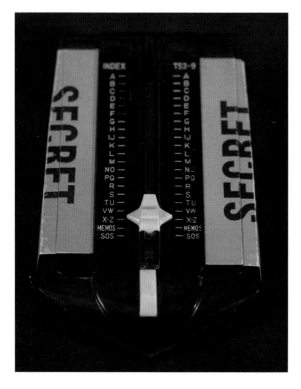

This spring-loaded teledex (telephone index) was referred to during the Hope Royal Commission on Intelligence and Security in 1974. They were popular items during the 1960s and the Dohertys owned one just like it. Many of the names in the Doherty teledex were in code. (Courtesy of the National Archives of Australia, NAA: A12404, 8)

This photo of a Brisbane May Day march was taken by socialist campaigner Grahame Garner. The image on the float is of a young man being held in a headlock by two police officers. Dudley Doherty would have been there taking photos as well. He and his family never missed a May Day procession. (Grahame Garner Collection, F3400, Folder 5, item 133, Fryer Library, The University of Queensland Library)

Protesters in the crowd at Festival Hall in Brisbane where Prime Minister Sir Robert Menzies was speaking on 23 April 1963. Dudley was probably there for ASIO, recording details of the known communists at the gathering and other 'persons of interest'. (Photo by Noel Pascoe, Newspix)

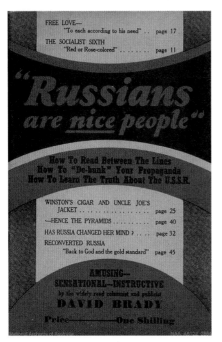

This pro-communist pamphlet was among documents seized by police when they raided Marx House, the Communist Party headquarters in Sydney, in June 1949. ASIO used these documents to help identify communists. (Courtesy of the National Archives of Australia, NAA: 6122, 2864)

Meanwhile (*above and below*), the government issued its own publicity to counter the communist threat. (Courtesy of the National Archives of Australia, NAA: 6122, 2864)

Fight Communism with —

TEN COMMANDMENTS
OF CITIZENSHIP

1. HOLD FAST TO YOUR HERITAGE OF FREEDOM.

2. BE BRITISH AND AUSTRALIAN FIRST.

3. BE TOLERANT OF ALL RACES, NATIONALITIES AND RELIGIONS.

4. PRACTISE YOUR OWN RELIGION SINCERELY.

5. BE NOT DECEIVED BY THE PROPAGANDA OF FOREIGN AGENTS.

6. BEWARE OF THE COMMUNIST WOLF IN SOCIALIST CLOTHING.

7. KNOW YOUR GOVERNMENT AND THE ISSUES BEFORE IT.

8. JOIN AND TAKE INTEREST IN YOUR POLITICAL ORGANISATION.

9. GUARD YOUR CHARTER OF FREEDOM — THE CONSTITUTION.

10. EXERCISE YOUR FREE RIGHT TO VOTE BOTH IN PARLIAMENTARY AND UNION ELECTIONS.

During the 1956 Olympics, Russian defectors Vladimir and Evdokia Petrov were sent on a Gold Coast holiday with the Dohertys, to keep them safe. Pictured are (*left to right*): Vladimir Petrov with fishing rod, Joan Doherty, Mark Doherty, 'Peewee' (Evdokia) Petrov with Sue-Ellen, and an unidentified ASIO officer.

Joan Doherty and Peewee Petrov played Chinese chequers during their Gold Coast holiday. They enjoyed talking about fashion, food and sex.

Vladimir Petrov, former Colonel in the Soviet intelligence service, fishes in the Nerang River on the Gold Coast with Mark Doherty. Sue-Ellen watches on. Joan had warned her not to go too close to Petrov.

Petrov made some friends when he caught a flathead during his Gold Coast holiday.

Peewee Petrov teases the proud fisherman in one of their friendly moments.

Sue-Ellen and Mark loved feeding the poddy calf at a farm they regularly visited when their parents met with an ASIO colleague outside Brisbane.

When the ASIO lift driver, Mr Buchanan, went on holidays to Maroochydore, he invited the Dohertys to stay for a couple of rare, carefree days. Sue-Ellen is 8 and Mark is 9.

Sue-Ellen and her good friend Leigh Rowland on holidays together at Mittagong with Grandma Doris and Grandpa Jack. They often entertained themselves by playing dress-ups.

Mark, Sue-Ellen and Amanda at Kilmaine Street, The Gap, in 1967.

Sue-Ellen participated in the Miss Personality Quest in 1972 and her prize was a trip to Hayman Island. During her holiday, she won the 'chopstick-eating competition'—one of the skills she had acquired during her unusual childhood.

Lorraine, Aaron (Dweezel) and Erich Saikovski in their house in Glebe, at the time when Sue-Ellen lived with them in the 1970s.

One of the few pictures taken at the wedding of Sue-Ellen and Hugh. (*Left to right*): Mark, Sue-Ellen, Hugh and Amanda, who cried all through the service and afterwards as well.

Sue-Ellen and Hugh on a Christmas holiday in Adelaide soon after their wedding.

Phoebe with Sue-Ellen in Bulimba during the 1980s, around the time when Sue-Ellen made a police report about a man in a car.

After Dudley died, the family lost all contact with old friends from ASIO. But on a couple of rare occasions 'Uncle Mick' would make an appearance. Here he is (*above*) with Sue-Ellen (*left*) and Amanda at Joan's 60th birthday party.

Joan (*right*) in 2020, now living in a nursing home in Brisbane.

Amanda, Mark and Sue-Ellen (*below*) in 2020.

Joan's well-polished story of her childhood—the homemade ice cream, the veggie garden, the country hospitality—had too many gaps. Her brave story concealed a very different reality. The Ridgways had kept up appearances. They always made visitors comfortable, but only at great cost to the family. When Joan had walked out of her father's house at sixteen, only months after she met Dudley, she had promised herself she would never go back. And she never did. She supported herself for four years before she married Dudley. They were in love, but Dudley did not feel free to marry her without his grandmother's blessing.

Joan had tried to forget about the time before she left her parents' home and, in the busy, hopeful early years of her marriage, she had succeeded. After hearing of her father's death, however, she was helpless to stop the memories of the old house at Liverpool surging up, filling her head, taking the place of sleep on long restless nights.

Oh, she had barely been able to wait to get away from that place. Of course there was always food to entertain visitors, but who milked the cow, who dug up the veggies, who cooked in their sweatbox kitchen? She did. Joan did it all, however hot the day, even if she was sick. And Clair, the sister she was close to, worked too, endlessly cleaning, polishing and shining their few things, washing the cleaning rags, scrubbing the floors. Harry, their surly Lancashire father, barked out commands. He had been a soldier in the British Army and had military standards of perfection in household tasks. When he went out, Leah, the beauty queen named after her mother, got out her movie books, lay back and gave out orders. The older girls ruled the roost in that house.

The skirts and button-down blouses Joan wore were all hand-me-downs from the other three girls. So were her Mary Jane shoes, with the strap across the front—they never quite fitted properly. Even her underclothes were hand-me-downs and the elastic was always saggy. Dudley knew how much she had hated that. That was why he gave her lovely underwear in white boxes tied with ribbons.

Joan's mother tried her best, but the work and the heat and the poverty were too much for her. Joan came home from school one day and found her sitting on a butter box in the middle of the kitchen, crying. Some men had come to take away the furniture because she couldn't afford to keep up the payments on it. It was the Depression and Joan's father may have been out of work then.

Of course, Joan's father had doted on her mother. Everyone said so. He never raised his voice to her, the way he did to the girls. He was gentle with her. But the way Joan described her parents' relationship was this: 'If he had said to her "Don't walk beside me—walk two paces behind", she would have done it without a murmur.' Harry was the boss of the family and no one ever questioned it.

Joan's father was a metal worker and the steel seemed to have got into his voice and his face and his hands. He gave orders and expected obedience—or else. If they didn't finish their chores or they talked back, his hand moved fast to his belt. Thrashings were hard and frequent, especially for Joan; she liked to talk back, though he said she was his favourite.

Harry had a shed in the yard where he fixed broken things and did some welding. He kept all the tools clean and neat. It was his kingdom and everything was in order. There was a particular smell there, of oil and rags and old wood. And personal smells. The smells of a man. After Joan heard of her father's death, it was the smells in that shed that haunted her, that rose up and choked her in the night.

He used to catch her at her chores and beckon her with an imperious curl of the index finger. No words—just a silent demand. It started when she was very little. The first time she thought it was special to be invited to his shed. She skipped down the hill after him. He wanted her to do special things for him. He was taking off his belt again, but not to hit her. He was showing her what he wanted with curt gestures and a few words. She wanted to please him. She was kneeling down, trying to please her daddy. She didn't like it but he put his hand on her head and held her down. He made ugly grunting noises, like a pig. She tried to please him, but he hurt her.

Nothing was special in her life again—until she met Dudley.

Years later, Joan found out that he had done the same thing to her sisters, but by then they were fully grown and it was too late for them to help each other. She never knew if her mother had known that her husband—that proud family man who loved his wife—had been abusing their daughters all those years. The family was splintered, broken. Her mother and her sisters became separated and scattered, each trying to forget, some of them drinking, some marrying cruel men.

Now Harry was dead. He had got away with it. There would be no explanations, no apologies, no revenge. There were just these wakeful nights, fighting off the memories, the smell of the shed that seemed to be trapped in her nostrils, making her gag. She couldn't forgive and she couldn't forget, and she couldn't take an axe and cleave him down the centre with one mighty blow.

Brisbane, 1959

Sue-Ellen is in the back of the Holden with Mark and baby Amanda. Dad is driving along a hilly street in town. She has been here before with Dad. They come here often to watch people going in and out of the union place, called Trades Hall. But today they are not going to the union place. They are going to a hospital because Mum is there. Dad parks the car up the hill from there and points high up in a tall brick building to a barred window.

'Mum's inside there,' he says. 'I'm going to see her. You two wait here.'

Sue-Ellen sits very still and waits. Mark reads his comic book. He is eight years old and he is always reading. Sue-Ellen is six and she doesn't like reading. She likes climbing trees and running around and shouting. But she knows she can't do that. When they are in the car, she has to be very quiet.

She doesn't know why Mum is in the room with the bars on the windows, except that Dad says she is sick. But she knows she can't ask any questions. She has to sit very still and wait. Soon, if she is very good and quiet, her mum will be better and will come home. When she gets back she will remember Sue-Ellen's name again and she will look after her like she used to.

Sue-Ellen sits very quietly and stares hard at the window, just in case her mum appears.

It must have worked, being so good and watching so hard, because Mum comes home again. Sue-Ellen hears Grandma Doris saying that Joan has had shock treatment. Grandma Doris is whispering and Sue-Ellen knows it is no use asking what 'shock treatment' is. Her grandma never answers her questions. But Sue-Ellen hears her say it is a miracle.

Even though Mum comes home and remembers them all again, she still isn't well. She has to rest, and so does Amanda, the baby. Sue-Ellen has to be good and quiet and it is very hard. She and Mark stay outside all day. She doesn't mind that because they play in the sandpit or climb trees. Or they go across the road to Jubilee Park and play on the swings. That's fun.

During her third pregnancy, Joan was unwell, her head bursting with migraines. When Amanda was born in February 1958, Joan collapsed. She was hospitalised with a form of postnatal depression that was so acute she temporarily forgot who she was. There was no need for her to keep secrets because she had forgotten them all.

Despite Dudley's faithlessness, Joan liked to believe that they were equal partners, that she wasn't submissive like her mother, or her sister Clair who was married to a bully. Or like Doreen Saffron. Joan knew she had a lot more spirit than they did. 'Doreen was just a wife for show, really,' Joan liked to tell her adult children. 'She had to follow orders from Abe like an employee.'

Joan made sure that her children did not suffer what she and her sisters had endured. They were safe with their father. And they never knew shameful poverty. The children laughed at

Joan sometimes for being a snob, for her insistence on perfect elocution and manners. But Joan worked hard and made sure her children didn't have to sit by while the bailiffs took their furniture. And she defended them from dirty old men—which is how she saw 'Jack' Petrov—and from anyone else who might take advantage of them.

Joan thought she could change the cycle of pain with her loving marriage, her good food and her beautiful home, and by watching her children like a hawk, keeping them chaste and alert. But she couldn't protect them from everything.

Sue-Ellen still has physical problems today caused by her mother insisting that she always keep her knees together. She sees a physiotherapist regularly. 'Mum was so strict about it. When I got older and went out on dates, she would give me these suspicious looks when I got home and ask me careful little questions. I didn't know what it was all about. Dad always said there was no need to know anything about sex because my husband would teach me everything I needed to know when I got married. That's why it was so weird later on, after Dad died, when all the rules suddenly changed.'

Sixteen-year-old Sue-Ellen knew about her mother's abuse at the hands of her father. Joan's rage—about her father's attacks on her, and about Dudley's cheating—had spilled out to the only person listening: her daughter. It was too much information for a girl who had been so protected and who was innocent in a way it's hard to imagine today. Sue-Ellen knew these facts of her mother's life, but she couldn't compute them. They were just more things that she became adept at shutting away in that box in her mind.

Later, Sue-Ellen came to see how Joan's childhood influenced her determination to be open with the children about their ASIO work. Joan had grown up in a family that had kept the secret of Harry's brutal abuse. Each of the daughters suffered alone. If they had spoken the truth, they might have been able to change something, or at least to support each other. As a mother, Joan wanted to be sure there were no secrets in her family. In any family that's a tall order, but in an ASIO family it is impossible.

14

Mystery Woman

Sydney, 1974

Sue-Ellen woke up to find Hugh wide awake, watching her. It had been a hot night and she was naked under a light sheet.

'Who are you, mystery woman?' Hugh asked her.

'There's nothing else to know, mate,' she smiled sleepily, stroking his face. 'You've seen the lot.'

'Ah yes. I know your body and I think I know your name. But who really are you? Did you just rise out of the sea in a shell? Who are your parents? Where did you come from?'

His voice was light, jokey. His hand lay gently on her stomach, but he was interrogating her. His eyes held hers and she could see him weighing up the evidence she had given him about her life, and finding it had no substance.

Hugh was not the usual twenty-three-year-old apprentice. His first career, at the age of seventeen, was as a chalkie on the boards at the Stock Exchange—to the dismay of his scientist parents. That was the time of the 'Poseidon bubble', when the value of mining shares soared. Hugh made a lot of money in 1969, and then lost it all in 1970 when the bubble burst. He quit the boards and went to trade college to become a manufacturing jeweller. His work was promising enough for him to be offered a Churchill Fellowship at the age of 21 to learn silversmithing skills in Britain. Jewellery design was his answer to the question of how to make an honest living, independently, with beauty at the centre of it. He was an unconventional man, willing to take risks in life, but he liked to assess the odds clearly.

Sue-Ellen saw he was serious. 'Why does it matter?'

'It doesn't matter if we don't matter, if this is a passing thing. Is that what it is?'

She sat up against the pillows and took his hand. 'We matter,' she said. 'Can we talk about it later, with our clothes on?'

⌒

Sue-Ellen dressed carefully to tell Hugh her story. She had always known the importance of clothes in creating an identity. She put on a simple summer dress and sandals, no jewellery and little make-up. She wanted him to see her as she was.

They had dinner at the restaurant where they had had their first date, the little Italian place with the gingham tablecloths, which was their comfortable, familiar haunt now.

When the minestrone was steaming on the table in front of them, Sue-Ellen looked around carefully, and leaned forward, speaking more softly than usual.

'My father was an ASIO spy,' she said.

'Really?' That wasn't what Hugh was expecting. 'How did you find out?'

'We all helped him—Mum, Mark, Amanda and me. Even when we were very little, we used to help him with his work.' She lowered her voice even further. 'We had the Petrovs come to stay.'

'You were a child spy?' He kept his voice level. 'That must have been pretty weird.'

'It just seemed normal to us at the time.'

'Uh-huh,' he said, slowly. 'And is it okay for you to talk to people about it?'

'Oh no. I have never said a word. We would never do that.'

'But how did you keep secrets like that when you were little?'

'I had this box in my head. I pictured it as a kind of combination safe that I put all the dangerous secrets into. Once I put a secret into the box, it was safe. I never spoke about it to anyone. We were sworn to secrecy for life.' She leaned forward again. 'There's another thing you should know. Everyone thinks Dad is dead, even Mum, but I am pretty sure he's not.'

Hugh put down his soup spoon, buttered a piece of crusty bread with care, and looked at Sue-Ellen tenderly. 'Sweetie. I don't know what your dad did or why you're ashamed, but I don't care. If you don't want to tell me, you don't need to. You don't have to make things up.'

It had taken all her courage to tell him. She wanted him to be the one person in the world who knew who she really was. And he didn't believe her—not until many years after their wedding.

Sydney, September 1974

Thirteen guests came to the little stone church in Watsons Bay. That was all the people in the world they cared about and a couple more.

Joan had come down from Brisbane the night before with Mark, Amanda and Mark's wife Bron. The Sydney guests included Hugh's parents, Alexander and Mary, who were cautiously happy for the young couple, and Erich and Lorraine Saikovski, with Dweezel, who were elated. Hugh's best friend Roland was invited and he brought a surprise guest with him, a girl he hoped to impress. Hugh and Sue-Ellen had two boarders, Rod and Judy, at their house in Gladesville and they were also invited. Sue-Ellen's best friend Rita flew in from Adelaide. She brought a special wedding gift for Sue-Ellen—a pair of red platform shoes, six inches high, that she had bought in Italy during a working holiday in Europe.

The night before the wedding, Joan and Sue-Ellen sat alone together in the little kitchen, while Hugh was in his workshop, making Sue-Ellen's wedding ring.

'Do you know what you're doing?' Joan asked her daughter, holding both her hands in hers.

'No,' said Sue-Ellen. 'I have no idea.'

'Well, you don't have to go through with it.'

'I know, but it's okay. We can always change our minds.'

'Marriage doesn't really work that way, sweetie. You need to know it's what you want.'

Sue-Ellen put her head on Joan's shoulder, a little girl again, and then sat up straight.

'Mum, I don't know anything, but I love him, and I want to go ahead.'

The next morning was mayhem. Sue-Ellen got up early to go to the market for the wedding flowers. She made little natural bouquets for herself and for Amanda, her bridesmaid. Hugh's mother surprised her with the delivery of six cartons of magnificent azaleas from her garden. They were heavenly, but Sue-Ellen needed to find vases and arrange them all before she dressed.

Hugh went to the airport to pick up Rita, but she brought home the wrong suitcase. That was a disaster because Sue-Ellen was planning to wear the towering red shoes at the wedding and now they were circling forlornly around on the luggage carousel. Hugh sped back to the airport to swap the cases before coming home in time to finish making the wedding ring before the ceremony.

The dress was quirky and subtle, designed by Erich to display Sue-Ellen's curves. In the decade of peasant-style lace wedding dresses and crocheted gowns, Erich had created a figure-hugging dove-grey satin crepe dress for her, in a twenties style. Sue-Ellen had made a hat to wear with it—a little pillbox number with a red feather and red net over the face. Rita painted the bride's nails fire-engine red and brought her a lipstick to match. Amanda looked magnificent in a red dress too.

Finally, Sue-Ellen had arranged the last azalea and blotted her lipstick for the twentieth time. Rod, the lodger, handed her into his little vintage MG with Amanda helping her fold her dress inside. Rod drove to the church at top speed but, when they arrived, he wouldn't let her out of the car.

'Are you sure you want to marry Kusher? You can change your mind,' he said, as he drove an extra lap around the little turning circle in front of the church.

'Yes, yes,' she assured him.

'Are you really, really sure?' He kept driving in circles.

'Yes, Rod!' she roared. 'Stop the bloody car!'

Inside, she saw Hugh waiting for her, in a grey tweed suit with a tartan tie. He was so handsome, and there was love and joy in his eyes. She was filled with confidence. It was crazy, but they were doing it together.

Her confidence vanished a few minutes later when she found herself making promises of lifelong fidelity—in front of God and these people who knew her intimately. Handsome men like Hugh were not faithful; they didn't stick around. It would be safer to make no commitments, to get out while the going was good. And what about her promise to her dad?

She felt sick. She wanted to run out the door. Nobody knew it, though. She stood her ground and spoke her vows clearly and calmly.

As she turned around with Hugh to walk out the door, she cast one quick, hopeful look to the back of the church. Who was that tall man standing quietly near the entrance? His back was to her now and he was walking out the door. Was it him? Had he come for her wedding after all?

Outside the church, there was no sign of the man. The glorious sunny morning had changed into an unseasonably cold afternoon, with a freezing wind. The sky was black; there was thunder and lightning. The group stood shivering beside the cliffs at South Head. Luckily they didn't have to pose for photos because Roland was the photographer and his camera was broken.

They all piled into taxis to go to the North Sydney Travelodge for dinner. Sue-Ellen had arranged dinner and a very good deal on a hotel room through a friend in the industry. After the reception, Sue-Ellen and Hugh stayed there while the rest of the guests returned to the Gladesville house and partied riotously all night, with Joan leading the fun.

When Hugh and Sue-Ellen came home the next day, they found their home a mess of empty champagne bottles, over-flowing ashtrays and food-encrusted plates, with the bodies of friends and family comatose on beds, sofas and cushions in all corners of the tiny house. They spent their one-day honey-moon cleaning up the house and cooking their guests a huge breakfast of bacon and eggs. And they couldn't stop laughing, with relief and joy.

Joan remembered a day, twenty-five years earlier, when she had sobbed over the uneaten cakes she had cooked for her reception. She was proud to see that, amid all the chaos and unpredictability of her daughter's wedding, Sue-Ellen was part of a loving group of family and friends.

15

Sue-Ellen's Secret Life

Brisbane, 2000

Sue-Ellen Kusher walked briskly down Queen Street among the morning office workers. The standard business look in this former British, subtropical town was dowdy comfort. Running shoes with suits were acceptable on the street, with a pair of scuffed court shoes in a drawstring bag to slip on at the office. Some women chose not to bother with businesswear at all and wore loose cotton dresses with sandals to beat the heat. Sue-Ellen couldn't bring herself to wear running shoes or cheap sandals—she had a love affair with good footwear. But she fitted in quite well with the Brisbane crowd in a plum-coloured suit with modest heels.

In her glory days in Sydney, her blonde bob would have been twisted into a confection of braids, her shoes would have been purple-and-green brocade scuffs to match her glasses, and her make-up would have been bold and luscious. Now her clothes were plain and tailored—linen, silk or high-thread-count cotton—and her shoes were comfortable and quietly elegant. People could see her, but they didn't notice her.

They couldn't see what she was doing.

Sue-Ellen was following a man. He was a tall, well-built man in a suit. She saw him from across the road. Without any appearance of indecision or changing her route, she stepped confidently across the street and walked innocently behind him. She knew how to follow people without them knowing—her dad had taught her how to do it.

It was not the first time she had followed a man on the street, though this was the first time in a long while. She needed to get close enough to her target to see what she was looking for. Did he have a mark on the back of his neck—quite a distinctive mark where the creases of the skin crisscrossed?

Her father had had a mark like that on his neck. If she saw it, she would know it was him. Of course, she wouldn't speak to him while he was working, but she would know he was alive. And he would know she knew, and that she was protecting his cover. He would be proud of her for following him so skilfully.

She got close enough to see the man's neck was thick, red and unmarked. It wasn't him. Her heels click-clicked as she crossed at the next set of lights, a busy consultant on the way to meet a new client.

Sue-Ellen was still married to Hugh and, to her own surprise, it had turned out well, though it had taken a while.

They stayed in Sydney at first. She had quit her first career as an actress because she was always cast as the French maid, wiggling around in a figure-hugging black dress with a frilly apron. Sue-Ellen wanted to be a person, recognised for her competence, not just her tits and arse. She had moved into the travel industry, where she managed big international conventions. But in business, as in theatre, women automatically took second place, and she wasn't given the title of manager.

'And you are just the same!' she shouted at Hugh, when he put a deposit on a new house without telling her. 'You can't make a decision like that without talking to me.'

Hugh tried to treat her the way she wanted to be treated, but he found it hard to figure out sometimes. Sue-Ellen was hard to read. She had been brought up to withhold her opinions and to always fit in with what other people were doing. As a child she could be noisy and showy, but she could never say what she wanted. So Hugh often didn't know what she needed until she got frustrated and yelled at him. Twelve months after their wedding, sick of the rows, Sue-Ellen left Hugh and went to live with Joan in Brisbane, who took her in without comment.

This is how Hugh won her back: he let her go. He sent the car after her on the train and he sent her all the cash they had, to make it easy for her. He waited six weeks and then he called her.

'You stood in front of your family and promised to try, and you didn't,' he said. He knew that a promise was a solemn thing to Sue-Ellen and she couldn't argue with that. And she was missing him. She agreed to try again; he booked her a flight home and he met her at the airport. She walked up to him, half-shy, half-defiant.

'Where is your wedding ring?' he asked her.

'It's in my bag.'

'Put it on and show you mean to seriously try and make this work. Otherwise I'll book a plane back to Brisbane for you right now.'

She put on the ring.

In the end it was all right. They learned each other's ways. A few months later, Joan came down to check for herself how things were going.

'I like him,' Sue-Ellen told her over breakfast. She had taken a day off but Hugh had gone to work. 'I like his mind. We don't hide things from each other and we have very good conversations. If I ever say I want to do something, he says, "What's stopping you?" And he's kind, Mum. He's gruff and cranky but he's genuinely kind. I can't resist that.'

Joan listened keenly and nodded. 'That'll do then, love. He's a keeper.'

~

Twenty-five years later, Sue-Ellen and Hugh were living in Brisbane with their three children: Lachlan, Cameron and Phoebe.

Hugh was in business and Sue-Ellen was a consultant, teaching leadership skills in big corporations. They lived in a large Queenslander home in a pretty riverside suburb. The house was surrounded by a quarter-acre of gardens with neatly trimmed hedges and orchids, and a grand jacaranda tree in the front. Inside, the rooms were full of light, shining wood tables, comfy chairs and original art on huge canvases. Scattered family photos showed Sue-Ellen and Hugh with the three children, looking relaxed, sometimes laughing, arms slung warmly around each other. Verandahs gave alternatives of sun or shade to sit with coffee and papers, all year round.

Anyone visiting Sue-Ellen would have said she was the whole package: prosperous, enviable, radiating wellbeing like a woman in an instant-coffee ad. Her confidence was superb.

No one but Hugh knew that her confidence was fake.

Only Hugh knew that, since her forty-seventh birthday, Sue-Ellen had pretty much given up sleeping. She woke each night from sweaty nightmares and left their bed. At dawn, he would find her huddled in the corner of the big couch in the living room. He stopped asking her what was wrong. She always said, 'I had a dream about Dad.' He had nothing new to say to that. He would sigh, put a reassuring hand on her shoulder, and go back to bed.

Dudley Doherty had been forty-seven when he disappeared. When Sue-Ellen turned the same age, he started to appear in her sleep. He would be sitting on his bed, assembling himself for the day, strapping on his wooden leg, already clear-eyed and efficient, with a grin and a joke for her when she put her head around the door. She would be happy to see him. She would open her mouth to tell him she had been flying when, still asleep, she would realise she'd been dreaming.

Desolation would wash over her, and then fear. Where was he now? Sue-Ellen would push herself to the surface of her dream, wake and shuffle with heavy feet out to the couch to wait for morning.

Since her birthday, it had become harder to keep things separate. Memories were leaking out of that box in her mind, even when she was awake. During those early-morning hours on the sofa, in a sleeping house, urgent questions tormented her. Could her father really be alive? And if he was, what did that mean? What sort of man would abandon his family and keep them waiting all these years, with no contact or communication?

Of course, she wondered whether she was mad. She knew other people would think so, if she told them about her secret life. She didn't even tell Hugh about following men on the street who might have been her father. He had never believed that Dudley might still be alive. It had taken nearly a decade after their marriage for him to believe that Dudley had been a spy. While they were living in Sydney, he had thought Sue-Ellen had been deluded by Joan, whom he privately considered to be a 'fruitcake'. When they went to Brisbane and he got to know Amanda and Mark, little things were said and done over the years that finally verified the ASIO story for Hugh, but Sue-Ellen was sure he would question her sanity if she told him how much she still waited and watched for her father to return.

Occasionally a friend would mention that they were seeing a therapist and Sue-Ellen would note down the name of the person they were seeing. How wonderful it would be to talk to a kind, clever shrink who would help her make sense of it all. But she never made an appointment. She could never experience that kind of relief. She was sworn to secrecy and, in an ASIO family, a vow is a vow and a secret is a secret—you don't get to talk to a therapist or a friend or even a priest. If she was mad, she was going to have to live with it somehow, and keep it hidden.

But maybe she wasn't mad. Other spies had left home suddenly and turned up in the Soviet Union. Her father was a disappearance artist—that was a fact. So maybe he was alive. Maybe he was a celebrity in Moscow right now, tucking into a tub of caviar with Harold Holt.

Sue-Ellen's confidence in her memories was confirmed by a curious incident in which she unconsciously tapped into her childhood training. One day, she and her little girl walked from home to the local shop in Bulimba to buy milk. Three-year-old, golden-haired Phoebe held her hand and talked non-stop. She was excited because she wanted to play the Pac Man game just outside the shop. You had to put money into the machine to play, but Phoebe didn't know that. She just pressed the buttons and thought she was playing.

Out of the corner of her eye, Sue-Ellen saw a light-blue car slowing down on busy Oxford Street and pulling in to park. A man got out and strolled slowly down the opposite side of the street. Sue-Ellen wasn't looking at him, but she knew he was watching them. Sue-Ellen kept hold of Phoebe's hand as she went into the shop, but Phoebe said, 'Please, Mum, can I play Pac Man?'

'Okay,' said Sue-Ellen cautiously, 'but you have to stand exactly here and not move. I need to be able see you the whole time.' She went into the shop to buy milk. While she was paying for it, she saw out of the corner of her eye that the man had crossed the road diagonally and was walking towards the shop. She felt rather than saw his shadow moving towards the shop, towards Phoebe. She threw her purse onto the counter at the shopkeeper and ran outside to grab her daughter and bring her inside. The man backed off, returned to his car and drove away.

She walked home calmly but, when Phoebe was playing in her room, Sue-Ellen broke down and started to cry. She told Hugh what had happened.

'You need to report that to the police straightaway,' he said.

'No! They'll think I'm nuts.'

'It's not just you—it's the accumulation of these stories that help the police to build a case,' said Hugh. 'You don't know what else this guy has done. Ring them.'

She did, and two police officers arrived within minutes. Sue-Ellen sat down with them and the policewoman took out her notebook and said, 'Tell me what happened.' Sue-Ellen told them exactly what had occurred and the policewoman looked astonished.

'Why do you think you noticed him?' she asked.

'Because he was behaving unusually,' said Sue-Ellen.

'How?'

'Well, he drove down the street at the pace we were walking, and he parked the car, but he didn't stop looking at us.'

As Sue-Ellen told the story, she was able to describe the man's appearance, the make and numberplate of the car, where he parked, what direction he drove off in, at what point precisely he stopped watching them. She didn't even know she knew these things until she answered the questions. The policewoman gave her another amazed look and Sue-Ellen stopped talking.

'Is something wrong?' she asked.

'No. Keep going,' said the police officer. 'You're going fine. That's a really good report. We can do something with that information.'

Sue-Ellen's training had kicked in—all those days of remembering faces at marches and numberplates in driveways. Despite her fear, she had stayed calm in front of Phoebe and had recalled every detail of the man and the incident. If she had panicked, or remained unaware, the man might have got Phoebe. Sometimes her whole childhood seemed like a crazy dream, but that incident proved it had happened. So maybe it wasn't so crazy to think her father was alive.

It didn't help her sleep, though. Staring blankly at the window one night, Sue-Ellen realised she could see the feathery leaves of the jacaranda floating in the breeze. Oh god, the sun was up. She had been awake all night and now she had to get ready for work.

She couldn't go on like this. For thirty years she had lived a double life, but now it was splitting her apart. She needed to know once and for all whether her father was dead or alive. Who was this man she had been waiting for all these years? And did he love her, Sue-Ellen, his first daughter? Or was she just another person he had charmed and used?

It was important to know. There were two Sue-Ellens. The private Sue-Ellen had dedicated her life to waiting for her father, to being ready to drop everything and help him in his work at a moment's notice. And the public Sue-Ellen was connected to the private one. She might have done different jobs, lived a different life, if she had been certain he was dead. She had turned down promising work opportunities that might have taken her overseas, because she thought he might come back and need her. When she cracked the mystery of Dudley Doherty, maybe she could live a simple, open, whole life—as herself.

16

ASIO Answers the Call

Brisbane, 2000s

And then suddenly she knew. She was drinking tea with her mother, alone in Joan's kitchen, when she asked the question.

'Dad really did die, didn't he?' she asked.

Joan had been waiting years for this moment. She had suspected all along that Sue-Ellen didn't believe her father was dead. 'Yes,' she said, looking Sue-Ellen in the eye.

'And you're sure?'

'Yes.'

'You couldn't have been fooled?'

'No.'

That short, quiet conversation ended Sue-Ellen's illusion. For whatever mysterious, unconscious reason, she was finally ready to know the truth. Believing he was alive all those years, at least in her secret self, had preserved her childish idea of him as a powerful hero, almost an immortal. Now it came to her as a revelation that her father was a man, not just her father. He was a person and she didn't know who he was. She knew the facts about his adultery now. But she hadn't taken in what that meant. What kind of a man would treat his wife like that? And what else was there to know? All those lies and disappearances—were they really just part of 'work'? Was he really a good, patriotic ASIO agent? She realised she would have to make an effort to find out what kind of man he was because people would lie. And then the people who knew him would die, and the history would die with them.

This was the beginning of Sue-Ellen's determined quest for facts about her father. It was almost impossible at first, because everyone who had known her father was either bound by secrecy or they just didn't know him beyond the superficial limits he established for his many contacts with people.

She started interviewing people who knew him well, like the old family friends they knew as Aunty Pearl and Uncle Roy.

'What was Dad really like?' she asked.

'He was a wonderful man and so kind,' Pearl told her. 'Did we tell you about the time Roy was out of work and he left a whole salmon in the fridge?'

'Yes, yes. But was he really kind or was that just part of his cover story?'

'Oh Sue-Ellen, give it a rest,' said Pearl. 'You worry too much.'

She tried to talk to Amanda and Mark about their childhoods, but they just shrugged and said they didn't remember much about those days. After all those years of secrecy, of not speaking about things, you just forget. Anyway, what was the fuss about? Dudley Doherty was their dad. They had loved him, and they still did. He was just who he was.

No matter who she spoke to, she felt she was just getting platitudes. Nobody could tell her what her dad had valued or how he justified right and wrong to himself, or even what his private political opinions were. Nobody knew if he really believed in religion. Too many things didn't fit together. Yes, there was evidence that he was kind and good, but he had cheated on her mother and he had beaten Sue-Ellen when she was just a kid. He was best friends with one of Australia's biggest criminals, and he lied for a living. How did anyone know that he wasn't a double agent or a criminal just using ASIO as a cover story?

Sue-Ellen had been raised with strong ideas of right and wrong, goodness and justice. For the first time, she started to apply those principles to the man who had taught them to her. Once she dropped the idea that whatever her dad had done was automatically good, she wanted to know whether he had been bad.

In 2010, she phoned ASIO in Canberra, to ask if they would send her files about her father via freedom of information. She spoke to a nice man who said his name was Richard. He listened carefully, then said he was sorry not to be able to send her any files. He said she could call him again if she had other questions. *So you can refuse to answer those questions as well,* she thought, but didn't say it.

She thought about it some more and, a few days later, she rang the nice man again. 'I know you can't give me any phone numbers, but could you ask Uncle Mick to call me—Dad's partner at work?'

It must have been enough information to identify him, because the next day Sue-Ellen's phone rang. Uncle Mick's wife was calling to arrange for Sue-Ellen to meet him. Uncle Mick was very old then, close to death, and Sue-Ellen went to visit him in a nursing home. Amazingly, Mick's nursing home was just around the corner from her home in Brisbane, in the same suburb. It was more than twenty years since she had last seen him at Joan's sixtieth birthday party.

Mick was sitting up ready to talk to her. Behind him was a view out onto the eighth hole of the Bulimba golf course. Like all the ASIO men Sue-Ellen had ever met, he was charming. He invited her to sit on the bed and told her he was glad to see her as though he meant it. She felt comfortable and began to chat happily. She told him all about her life and her quest to find out more about her father.

'I remembered that you were Dad's partner, so I thought you would be the best person to ask.'

'He wasn't exactly my partner,' Mick said. She could see a small gold filling in one of his teeth as he spoke. 'I was the regional director for ASIO and he was the senior officer on my team.'

Finally! She had found someone who knew something. 'Oh, that's amazing,' she said. 'Can you tell me what Dad did at work?

'Sorry, Sue-Ellen—I can't tell you that because I never knew,' he said.

'But how could you be the director and not know what was going on?' she asked him, frustrated.

'That's how we kept secrets,' he said. 'Two men could be sitting next to each other and have no idea what the other was working on.'

'Wouldn't they ask each other?'

'No, no. It was secret, Sue-Ellen. Always secret.'

'Well, I think there were things about Dad you didn't know,' she told him.

Mick sat very still, waiting.

'I just don't know if he was everything we thought he was,' she continued.

He waited again. This time Sue-Ellen paused too.

'Sue-Ellen, do you think your father was a double agent?' he asked her. She saw he was troubled.

'No. No. But why was he friends with Abe Saffron?' she blurted out.

'Ah,' he said. 'I can see that would worry you. Well, don't worry too much about it. Your dad served our country well.'

After the first elation of having met her father's boss, Sue-Ellen realised she still didn't know much more than she had before. There was something those ASIO men did—she didn't know what it was—but people always ended up telling them everything and they never revealed anything in return. It had happened again. It seemed unlikely that she would ever find out anything real about her father.

⌒

It was at that point that Sue-Ellen, despairing of making any further progress on her own, decided to find a journalist who would help her track down the truth about her family. A mutual friend suggested I might be the right person to help her. She knew I was a former journalist, now working as an editor and corporate writing teacher, and writing in my spare time. Sue-Ellen and I had met a few times—at a wedding, a funeral and occasionally at lunch with a group. I liked her directness, her enthusiasm and what I thought was her openness, but I was surprised when she called and asked me for coffee. I could hear a beat of excitement in her voice and I was curious to know what she wanted.

She was drinking tea when I arrived at the little French cafe on Racecourse Road, Ascot, that she had suggested for our rendezvous. She looked at home in this old-money suburb with her blonde bob, a blue scarf that matched her eyes, funky heart-shaped glasses and perfectly applied make-up. When I sat down, she looked around carefully, leaned forward and spoke in a softer voice than usual. She told me briefly that her father had been a spy and that she herself had participated in Cold War spying activities.

I was intrigued, but I didn't believe her. Surely spies didn't involve their children in their work!

'Story of my life,' said Sue-Ellen, when I told her (much later) of my initial doubts.

The difficulty with this, or any other true-life spy story, is that there is no way to confirm any of the facts. ASIO was certainly not going to provide me with information; their job is to gather information, not to give it out. And I knew it was illegal to publish national secrets without permission from ASIO, and that they were never going to give it.

Sue-Ellen showed me a little black-and-white photo of her as a child with her parents. The idea of that little girl with the blonde plaits helping Daddy spy on communists was irresistible. It had never occurred to me that spying might be a family business. I wanted to know how that might work and what it would mean for the children in those families. Maybe, just maybe, it was true.

I arranged to meet her again. And again. As she gave me more and more details of her childhood, I began to believe her, but I could not write the story without being able to confirm any of the most basic facts. I had exactly the same problem as Sue-Ellen did—I had no way of knowing what was true and what was cover story, or even delusion. I put the story aside to work on other things.

Then, the following year, in 2011, the nice man called Richard rang Sue-Ellen.

'Hello Sue-Ellen,' said the easygoing voice, reminding her of their earlier conversation. 'ASIO is preparing an official history and we wondered if your mother would like to speak to the researchers. There are a couple of gaps in our files and we think she may be able to help us fill them in.'

'Yes, yes,' she said. 'I'm sure my mother would be glad to. Let me talk to her.'

She rang Joan immediately, bubbling over with excitement.

Joan was eighty-two; her ASIO life was four decades and one marriage behind her. But she hadn't forgotten the rules. She told Sue-Ellen that she absolutely would not speak to anyone without proof that they were from ASIO and high-level written proof that she was allowed to speak to them. Sue-Ellen passed on the message to her contact and they agreed unequivocally to Joan's terms. They made an appointment to visit Joan at her home in the pretty bayside suburb of Victoria Point on 8 April 2011.

They arrived on time. Three men stood on the doorstep, one of them carrying an enormous bunch of red roses. Maybe they took bouquets to everyone they interviewed, or maybe they knew that Joan had a special love of flowers—that detail would have been on file. Two of them were very senior and it is illegal to name them. The other one was Dr Rhys Crawley, a researcher then based at the Australian National University (ANU), who was working on the ASIO history.

Joan had remarried by this time. Her second husband, Roy, had recently moved into a nursing home, but Sue-Ellen made sure she was with Joan when the ASIO team arrived. She wouldn't have missed it, whatever she had to cancel. She made tea and put out biscuits.

Joan recognised one of the men as a former senior ASIO official from Dudley's time. He assured her that the attorney-general was behind the project, as was the prime minister, and that she was completely free to talk to them. Joan was still hesitant, but Sue-Ellen watched her relax when the men gave her a handwritten letter to read. Joan looked carefully at the signature and nodded to them to begin. The interview began with some gracious formalities from ASIO.

'On behalf of the Commonwealth Government, we want to thank you for the part you played in some of the most extraordinary events in Australia's history,' they said. 'Your contribution was remarkable and unique.'

Joan sat quietly as they congratulated her for several firsts in the history of Australian espionage.

Joan and Dudley had been part of the first ever clandestine surveillance exercise in ASIO. Joan had done top-secret work behind the Green Door in ASIO's first-ever bugging exercise. Joan and Dudley had sheltered defecting Soviet agents, Vladimir and Evdokia Petrov, during the 1956 Summer Olympics, and may have saved their lives.

The visitors said that, because the work Joan did was so secret, very little was known about it. They would appreciate her letting them know anything she remembered about those early days of ASIO's existence. Joan agreed to answer their questions to the best of her ability. The officials sat back quietly and allowed Rhys Crawley to lead the questions.

Sue-Ellen listened to all this with astonishment, her teacup frozen in mid-air. They wanted to know about her *mother*?

Joan had always said she worked for ASIO before the children were born, without discussing the details. Sue-Ellen had understood it was untrained clerical work, and that her father was the real spy. But these officials wanted to know about her mother's work, not her father's. They said she had made an important contribution to Australian security. Sue-Ellen had hoped to find out more about her father when she contacted ASIO; it had never occurred to her that she would also have to revise her opinion of her mother.

ASIO recorded the conversation with Joan. She talked clearly for more than three hours in her calm, well-modulated voice, giving details of operations as far back as 1950, the year she joined The Firm.

When Rhys Crawley had finished his interview, the most important person thanked Joan warmly and confirmed that she was no longer bound by secrecy on any matters they had discussed. If they could describe her career in a public book, Joan was also free to speak about it.

After they left, Joan was calm. She said, 'I always felt there was unfinished business with them, and now it feels finished.'

Sue-Ellen was full of large and contradictory feelings. She cried on and off for days afterwards, but mostly she felt relieved and happy. Her father had done valuable work for the country—and so had her mother. When something cannot be talked about, it is hard to believe it is real. Now there was no doubt about it.

Sue-Ellen is not a journal writer but that day she felt she had to put something on the record. 'I am completely overwhelmed by the power of having our story heard and acknowledged,' she wrote. 'I am so happy for my mother and my father. It's like there was a bloody big hole in the middle of our lives and now it has been filled. I can't believe it. It's so healing.'

She sent me an emotional email about the visit from ASIO. Finally, I had a definite lead. I phoned Rhys Crawley. He was working for ANU, not for ASIO, so he was free to confirm essential facts—and he did. He said that Joan's memory of her early days was formidable, and the precision of her answers was astonishing. He said it was a fascinating side story in ASIO's history.

Now we could begin work.

I agreed to help Sue-Ellen track down and understand the facts of her childhood, provided she would allow me to write

WITH MY LITTLE EYE

the story as I saw it. I had no interest in being a ghostwriter. Sue-Ellen accepted. She asked me to help her discover what was reality and what was illusion. What was a lie and what was true? Who were her parents—and could she trust them?

After the interview, ASIO disappeared from their lives until the first book in the ASIO history series, *The Spy Catchers*, was published in 2014. Joan and Sue-Ellen received handsome invitations for the book launch at Old Parliament House in Canberra. It never even occurred to Joan, living her quiet life, that she would accept the invitation, but Sue-Ellen insisted. 'Why not?' she said to her mother. 'This is never going to happen again.' She bought airline tickets; the day of the launch arrived, and Joan was greeting people who had been her colleagues more than sixty years before.

In a roomful of politicians and public servants, there were only six women and it was easy for Joan to find the other Joan, the one who had been her best friend back in those heady days at the beginning of ASIO. The two Joans had jointly run the ultra-secret operation behind the Green Door, transcribing the phone conversations of people whose names became world-famous during the 1954 Royal Commission on Espionage: the Petrovs, Michael Bialoguski, Fedor Nosov, Walter Clayton, and people with code names like 'TOURIST' and 'FERRO'. The two old friends sat together throughout the launch and gossiped about family members and colleagues and the little details of each other's lives, just as they had done in 1950.

There were speeches and a fine lunch and meetings with old friends, and Joan was happy and proud to be greeted by people who knew of her work and admired her.

Sue-Ellen was excited, but she had other feelings as well. 'Everyone there was such great friends with everyone else. They belonged to an ASIO community, whether they had retired or were widowed or whatever. Mum and I were the only ones there who had been cut off by ASIO and left to fend for ourselves. I was sad to think of all we had missed out on since 1970. It was quite a men's club, too. I felt like an outsider there.'

Joan was given a copy of the fat history book and she waited until she was alone to look at it. Her name and Dudley's were listed in the index, with short references to their work over five pages.

There was also a photo of Joan in 1956, in her bathing suit. She was posing for a holiday snap with Mark and Sue-Ellen, and with Jack and Peewee Petrov.

And that was that. ASIO had finished with them again and the topic was closed. At least it was closed for ASIO—the next volume of the history had no need for the Dohertys. It was closed for Joan, whose work had finally been acknowledged by the nation and, as a result, by her family. And it was closed for Mark and Amanda, who were pleased for their mother but saw it as ancient history. Their lives had moved on.

But for Sue-Ellen the whole thing had just opened up. She had wanted a record of the facts for her children and their children, and ASIO had taken care of that. Now she realised that was only the smallest part of what she needed. The cage of secrecy had been opened and she wanted to fly right out of it. She needed to discover everything she had missed in the years of silence.

Sue-Ellen was tormented by a sense of hidden things in her family. She still didn't know why her father was friends with Abe Saffron or whether he was really working every time he went away. Her questions about the character of her father remained, and now she needed to think about her mother in a new way. Who was she? *Really*? All the old memories Sue-Ellen had locked away were rattling in their box. She was like Paula Alquist in the movie *Gaslight*, wondering why the gaslights dimmed and brightened for no apparent reason. And then wondering if she was crazy when the rest of the family insisted there was nothing there.

ASIO, unsurprisingly, did not reply to my request for information about the Dohertys. By this stage it was clear that the only living sources of information about them were the family members themselves. The Dohertys had never spoken about the spying parts of their lives, even to each other, and now they were free to do so. Sue-Ellen agreed to set up interviews with her family members.

We spoke to Joan first. She knew Dudley better than anyone and she was part of his ASIO world. At eighty-five she was alive and lucid and—most importantly—Sue-Ellen said she had agreed to talk to us. On the way to my first visit with Joan, Sue-Ellen explained to me her mother's open-information policy. 'If you ask her a question, she tells you the truth. If you don't ask her, she won't tell you anything.'

Joan was a neat, white-haired woman who greeted Sue-Ellen with a kiss and a soft exchange of family news. She welcomed me courteously and, leaning on her stick, showed me around her home and garden. When we sat down to talk, while Sue-Ellen made tea, she gave the impression of being on duty: back erect, dignified, watchful and ready to answer questions within whatever her private limits were. For the first couple of meetings, she just parried my questions. When I asked whether she was glad to have permission to talk about her ASIO career, she said it was just ancient history. When I asked what working for ASIO had meant to her, she told me flatly that it was just a job. I began to be discouraged but, the third time we met, I asked the magic question: 'How did you meet Dudley?' From then on she began to talk freely, happy to speak about the man she called 'the love of my life'. We recorded several fascinating and surprisingly frank interviews about her life.

After that, the only other people who could help Sue-Ellen were her brother and sister. Only Mark and Amanda had experienced what she had. Only they truly knew about the weird world she had grown up in.

They had never talked about it. Not once. In most families, people talk about holidays they have been on or special occasions. They look at old photos and laugh. But because their family life was all mixed up with Daddy's work, it was all Top Secret.

Sue-Ellen asked Mark and Amanda again to help her piece together their past and make sense of it. They both refused again. They said they would be glad to help if they could, but told her that they really didn't remember anything much.

In the end she wore them down. All right, all right, they said. They'd join her (and me) for a chat about the past, just once, and Sue-Ellen would finally see how hopeless the whole idea was.

PART 3

THE FAMILY

17

The Deep Pleasure of Facts

Brisbane, November 2011

They met on Sue-Ellen's verandah. It was a sunny afternoon, but cool enough to sit out there on squatter's chairs as the shadows lengthened. Sue-Ellen had arranged the chairs in a comfortable circle and laid out nuts and fruit. She was nervous, even though it was just her brother and sister coming around for a chat about old times. They'd kept in touch over the years, met for birthdays and Christmas, but they didn't talk about anything except daily news about children and jobs. They had never talked about their old lives as spy kids, or the night of their father's death and the strange events that followed.

Mark walked in quietly and hugged her. He was known as 'The Colonel' in the Brisbane music world, with his pure white quiff of hair and triangular beard. The quiet, bookish boy grew up to host a blues radio show and play in a band, while earning his keep as an optometrist. When he started his blues program on Brisbane's Radio 4ZZZ in 1978, it offered a radical alternative to the kind of music played on mainstream radio. Just playing black music was an edgy thing to do in 1970s Brisbane. Mainstream DJs kept black artists to a minimum and played easy-listening black singers like Nat King Cole or Fats Domino, rather than R&B or blues or wilder rock 'n' roll singers like Little Richard. His program wasn't so openly radical that it would necessarily earn him an ASIO file, but it was clearly non-conformist. Dressed plainly in T-shirt and jeans, Mark was a retiring figure with a gentle manner, but Sue-Ellen knew that a powerful, analytical brain was working non-stop behind his mild expression.

They chatted about their mother, who was having trouble settling into a new retirement village. Mark and Sue-Ellen both kept an eye on Joan. They changed the topic when Amanda arrived; she had very little contact with her mother anymore. Amanda was a neat, self-possessed woman in her early fifties, with a well-cut bob and a pleasing face. Amanda's Pinterest page included the quote: 'Just because I don't react doesn't mean that I don't notice.' Sue-Ellen had seen it recently and snorted: 'That's for sure.' Amanda could easily play the role of Miss Marple— that acute, well-bred social observer who could find things out without people having any idea what they were giving away.

After a short bustle of making drinks and finding chairs, the three siblings sat down and looked at each other. Mark and Amanda had resisted this meeting. They didn't expect it to be fruitful. But they were good sports and, now that they were here, they would try to help. They knew it meant a lot to Sue-Ellen.

'Do you remember how Dad used to disappear?' Sue-Ellen asked.

'It was more of an event when he was there,' said Mark.

'He was never off work,' said Amanda, 'even if he was there.'

'Nope,' said Mark. 'There was always an agenda.'

'An ulterior motive,' said Amanda. 'We'd get a surprise if he took us to the Ekka'—the Royal Queensland Show—'but it would turn out there was someone he'd have to see. He'd leave us with Mum and go off somewhere.'

'How did you know he was meeting someone for work?' I asked.

They looked at each other, uncertainly. 'We just knew what was happening,' said Sue-Ellen. 'We put adult values on it later, but we always knew at the time.'

Suddenly they couldn't stop talking. They remembered the disastrous holidays, the car trips where they changed places, Dudley's dictaphone and the special keys he had, the way they couldn't talk to him after work. It all came spilling out. When Sue-Ellen mentioned the numberplate runs, Mark exclaimed: 'Yes, I'd forgotten! *That's* why I've got a fixation with numberplates.'

They marvelled at how the memories came rushing back and how they shared so many of them. They were excited, but they kept the perfect manners they had been raised with. They spoke quietly and factually, letting their siblings finish sentences without interrupting or speaking over each other. They listened and acknowledged each other with small courteous gestures. If they disagreed, it was in a thoughtful, testing way.

They worked together to assemble facts from their childhood, listing things and people.

'Call out all the names of the places we watched in the car with Dad,' said Sue-Ellen.

'Roma Street Parkland, for the demonstrations,' called Mark.

'And Queen's Park. Ditto.' That was Amanda.

'Kemp Place. Is that the name of it? You know, Speakers' Corner.'

'It was called Centenary Place.'

'There was a house in Samford. That guy was a waterside worker.'

'The terrace houses on Coronation Drive where the brothel was,' Sue-Ellen threw in.

'That house opposite the Princess Alexandra Hospital, except the hospital was called something different then.'

'Oh yes, and the belly dancer down at the bottom of Coorparoo.'

'Trades Hall.'

'And there was somewhere in the Valley where we used to go often and walk around the block in different groupings.'

Later in the afternoon:

'Can you remember the name of the woman Dad was having an affair with?' asked Sue-Ellen.

'Which one?' said Amanda.

'The Spanish one.'

'Was she the one on the boat?'

'No, she was the one who did the cooking at the Exhibition.'

'That's it! Maria.'

Mark looked startled.

'Does that surprise you?' asked Sue-Ellen.

'I obviously had blinkers on,' he replied.

'I found out when I was sixteen,' said Sue-Ellen.

'I didn't know till years later, though I knew there was something wrong,' said Amanda. 'Maria used to spoil me in a really over-the-top way. She gave me a gold cross and toys and a dress, but she didn't give presents to Mum or anyone else.'

'I guess everything was on a "need-to-know" basis,' laughed Mark.

'They were just "special contacts" Mum didn't need to know about,' Amanda quipped back.

This wry, apparently casual exchange about their father's mistresses was the way the Doherty kids dealt with difficult conversations. Each of them knew small fragments about their parents' lives and were uncertain of how much the others knew, of how important it was, or what it signified. Playing it cool was safe.

When coffee cups were replaced with wine glasses, Sue-Ellen asked if they remembered where they were when their dad had died. There was a short silence before they began to talk, each chipping in their own parts of a story they had never spoken of to anyone for forty-one years. They spoke as though it was happening now, vividly remembering the night that had ended their childhood and the strange events afterwards.

Brisbane, 18 October 1970

Dudley Doherty is dying at home. The family is not standing respect-fully around the bed, listening for Dudley's final words, as you might

177

imagine in a scene like this. In this family, nothing ever seems to happen like that, with everyone together, all seeing and hearing the same things. In this family, life is full of shocks and sudden disappearances and nobody sees the same thing, or remembers the same thing, as anyone else.

A few minutes before, Dudley had been eating his favourite meal of chicken and cashews from Johnny Go's Chinese restaurant at Windsor. Johnny is an ASIO contact, but now he is a friend too, since Dudley helped him find a wife to come out from China and did all the paperwork for the government to bring her out. Dudley never has to phone in an order. When Johnny sees him, his face creases with smiles. 'Hello, Mr Dorothy, I got something special for you today.' The Chinese contacts all have trouble saying his name. Big handsome Dudley, easy in his ways, genuinely interested, leans on the counter and asks Johnny about business and how his wife is, while Johnny packs him up his most succulent dishes in takeaway containers. Dudley always asks for the bill, but Johnny won't let him pay.

Dudley loves his food and he never leaves the table during a meal. But tonight he gets up suddenly from the dinner table and walks down the hallway. Joan runs after him. Twelve-year-old Amanda sees the fear in her mother's face and then hears her father's testy voice in the hall saying, 'Don't fuss.' Joan calls out sharply to Amanda: 'Phone the doctor.'

Amanda finds the number for their GP in the cream plastic teledex, flipping open the page at M. Some of the numbers are in code, but not the one for the doctor. She calls Dr McPherson but his wife says he is having dinner and he can't come yet. Now Joan shouts out: 'Get Mark.'

Amanda's brother, Mark, has a workbench downstairs. He is nineteen and very brainy. They call him 'The Mad Scientist' and it is not unusual for him to miss dinner if he is involved in some experiment.

Amanda calls down to him through the laundry chute but he doesn't hear her. She can hear her mother and father upstairs in their bedroom now, and she runs up, but her mother won't let her in, and won't tell her what is happening. 'Call the doctor again,' she orders.

Amanda tries the doctor's number once more. The doctor's wife says crossly, 'I've already told you. He's having his dinner.'

'I don't care,' says Amanda, desperate, forgetting her manners. 'I need him here. There's something wrong with my dad. You send him right now.' She slams down the phone.

She runs down the back stairs to find Mark. 'Mum wants you. There's something wrong with Dad.' Mark hears the panic in her voice. He pounds up the stairs and runs into his parents' bedroom. Amanda is behind him, but Joan snaps at her. 'Stay out, Amanda. Get the dog. Take her into your room and stay there until someone tells you to leave.'

The miniature dachshund, Honey, is devoted to Dudley and she knows something is wrong with him. She is protecting him the best way she can by biting anyone who comes near him on the bed.

Amanda picks up the biting, scratching, scrabbling dog and goes to her room. She has to hold Honey because the dog is going ballistic. Honey is scratching her, but Amanda obeys Joan without question, as the children always do. Her room is next door to her parents' and she hears everything through the walls. She hears her mother saying, 'Dudley, don't do this to me.' She hears some terrible, unidentifiable noises. Amanda is crying. She is praying, making bargains with God. She grips the struggling dog with all her strength. She just wants whatever is happening to stop.

Mark sees his father lying, blue faced, strained, gasping, on the bed. He sees Dudley open his eyes, searching for Joan, sees his hand creep *across the sheet to touch her hand. 'Always get your hair done, Jo Jo. Always take your tablets,' breathes Dudley. His last words.*

Then the pain takes over and Joan is kneeling beside him, blowing rhythmically into his mouth, then pounding on his chest. Dr McPherson finally arrives and Joan falls back, exhausted. Mark watches with horror as the doctor lifts a big needle high and jabs Dudley straight in the heart. Too late. A gurgling noise comes from Dudley's throat. Then he gives a great heave of breath, a final sigh, and Mark can see that his dad is not there anymore.

In the room next door, Amanda hears a moment of silence and a cry and then Joan is telling Mark to ring people, calling out phone numbers to him. It makes no sense to Amanda. Why is her mother making Mark call all these people?

People arrive quickly. Amanda hears footsteps, voices, little cries and sobs. Mark is not a drinker but somebody has given him a shot of scotch and he is on the phone ringing people and telling them what has happened. There are so many people to ring. So many people who knew Dudley and loved him. Contacts, police, agents—but all of them are his friends.

When Dudley was alive, their lives were full of people. It was so strange to think about it afterwards, when there was no one.

Mark is trying to stay calm, detached, to do what is needed. That monumental effort changes him; for the rest of his life, this sensitive boy holds on to the detachment he learns the night his father dies. People start arriving at the house. Their friend June Barton comes quickly. Grandpa Jack and Grandma Doris are here. Neighbours come to the door, shocked, trying to comfort Joan, who is crying. The house is full of people, but Amanda is still shut in with the dog and Mark is phoning, phoning.

Sue-Ellen is still not here. She is on a date and, when she gets back, it is too late.

Mark finally rescues Amanda. He is taking the dog, he is talking gently to Amanda, and she can hear his words but she doesn't know what he's saying. Nothing is making sense. Now he has gone again and she is huddled in the corner of her room. Their neighbour, Mr Duddie, comes in and picks her up. 'You're coming with me,' he says.

'Why do I have to go?' asks Amanda.

'Your mum said you should come to my place.' Mrs Duddie is there too and they take her home to sleep with their little girl, Kerry. Mr Duddie carries her all the way and she asks him what it all means. He says, 'Your dad is dead.' Even though Mark has told her, she needs to hear it again, even though it makes her cry and she knows nothing will ever be all right again.

As Amanda leaves, Sue-Ellen steps inside this weird house that used to be her comfortable, familiar home.

⌒

At 6 a.m. on the morning after Dudley died, two men in dark suits arrived on the doorstep of their house in The Gap. One of them looked familiar to Joan and he flashed an ID at her. She stepped aside to let them in.

Dudley had been a meticulous man. He had learned that precision while living with the Salvos as a young man. The family all knew he could get dressed in the dark—as he often did. He put everything away in the same order each night on his lowboy: wallet, change, keys, lock-picking kit. The last thing he did each night was to take off his wooden leg and lean it against the lowboy.

The two men searched swiftly and precisely. They collected Dudley's lock-picking equipment, his notebooks, his leather bag. They picked up the wooden leg and shook it out to see if anything was inside. Sue-Ellen was following them, crying, still in her nightie. Before they left, they reminded Joan she was bound to silence. They told Joan to line the kids up so they could instruct them to be silent, but Joan stopped them. 'These are my children and I am responsible for them. You are not talking to them.' They drove off in one of those regular Holdens from 1970—milky-coffee coloured, or pale green—the kind of car that was so insignificant you couldn't help noticing it, if you were an ASIO family.

That's what they had been until that moment: an ASIO family. So Joan did what an ASIO wife does. She called her shocked children and told them they must never speak about what they had seen that morning. Nor about anything that had happened in their lives as a spying family. It was their duty to be silent for the rest of their lives.

Sue-Ellen remembers that the strangers took Dudley's wooden leg with them—the leg that was as much a part of their father as his terrible jokes and his light-blue eyes. She remembers saying, over and over, 'They can't take that. That's Dad.'

Forty-one years later, Mark can't help her when she asks him if he remembers them taking Dad's leg. He just shakes his head slowly each time she asks. 'Sorry, Sue. I don't remember.'

And Amanda can't help because she wasn't there. She had to guess what was happening. She was watching her house from her exile at the Duddies' and she saw the car come and go in the early morning. She noticed it was like her dad's car. She was the unseen observer from over the road. She saw many other people coming and going from the house. Her grandparents came, bowed over. Their friends the Shun Wahs came, bringing boxes of Chinese food. Everybody could go there, except her.

Silence was a duty, but it was as though ASIO had put a curse on them. From that moment, each family member was alone, locked in with their own memories, their own grief, unable to talk about it with their closest family members or with anyone else.

Amanda has always felt that her family left her that night. 'I didn't have to leave my family. They left me,' she said in therapy, and later she got used to saying it and it became a dry joke, a little riff in her conversations with Mark and Sue-Ellen, when they could finally talk about it.

Mark's response was to forget everything that had happened. When his sisters asked him later about their childhood, he responded with a kind of litany: 'I don't remember. I don't analyse things. I just move on.'

Sue-Ellen simply decided it hadn't happened. She was used to things not being as they seemed and not making sense, and questions not being allowed. It didn't matter how many mourners were in the house drinking tea—she just didn't believe he was dead.

She asked to go to the funeral home to see for herself if it was her father. 'You don't want to do that,' said Joan. Normally, Sue-Ellen would have taken one of Joan's crisp suggestions as an instruction. If her mother thought she didn't want to do something, she accepted that she didn't. But this time she insisted. 'I do want to go,' she said. Finally, Mark agreed to take her, and Joan, with a flap of hands, gave in. They drove to the funeral home in silence and Mark stood quietly beside Sue-Ellen as she stared at the body.

Sue-Ellen saw the body, but she didn't believe it was her dad. It didn't look like him. He was grey and his lips were blue. And his wedding ring was so shiny. Everything else was dead except his wedding ring. It just glowed. It wasn't her dad. Sue-Ellen was shaking and crying and, when they left, Mark didn't drive her directly home. He drove up the winding road to the top of Mount Coot-tha and parked where the kissing couples went.

'What are we doing here?' asked Sue-Ellen.

'We're going to stay here until you're ready to go.'

His quietness and kindness calmed her. They sat together and Sue-Ellen thought it through. She knew that body on the funeral slab was not her dad. Her dad would not leave her like that. He was on a secret mission and she would keep his secret and wait for him to return. She would wait as long as it took. Decision made, she nodded at Mark and he drove her home.

From her watching post at the Duddies' window, Amanda could see flowers being delivered to her house several times a day. They kept coming and coming. Inside, there were no vases left, no jugs, no cups. There were too many flowers to keep in the house, so they started flowing out again. Joan sent flowers out to Mrs Gibson and Mrs Howell, and to the Loomas and the Duddies, and Amanda watched the flowers going in and coming out.

Joan held herself together for five days until the cremation at Albany Creek Memorial Park. She took her tablets, as Dudley had told her to do. There were some little orange-and-white capsules that kept her on an even keel at that time. She made arrangements about food and flowers. Joan had always been strong.

The funeral was huge. Only Amanda was not there. Sue-Ellen and Mark remember many people they had never met before, people of all nationalities, especially Chinese people and Yugoslavs. The flowers kept coming, including a giant horseshoe of flowers from Ray Whitrod, the new Queensland police commissioner. Joan put a simple bunch of carnations on the coffin—Dudley's favourite flowers, a symbol of their love. The Salvation Army's Brigadier Johns, who had cared for Dudley as a child in Sydney, was to give the service, but he was held up by flooding. The children agreed that the minister who replaced him could have been burying a fish.

Joan wore a red, white and blue crimplene dress. She had her hair done. She was beautiful and dignified; she stood at the door and thanked every single guest.

One month after Dudley's death, a woman called Pat knocked at the door of Joan's home. Joan recognised the pleasant, tanned woman with sandy-brown shoulder-length hair as the owner of the book exchange they visited each week with the children for books and comics. Dudley had made friends with her, as he did with everyone he met.

'I don't want to intrude,' she said to Joan, 'but Dudley sent me.'

'What on earth do you mean?' asked Joan.

Pat carried a bunch of carnations in one hand and a dried flower arrangement in the other. She presented them to Joan, then pulled a letter out of her handbag and handed that to her as well. 'He told me to bring you these,' she said.

'I don't know if I can deal with this,' said Joan.

'He wanted you to. Just read it,' said Pat.

Joan made tea for Pat. Serving food and drink to guests was non-negotiable for Joan, whatever she was feeling. You have to do what's right. They sat together at the table, with the tablecloth Joan had embroidered herself, and the floral tea set with a choice of Indian or Chinese tea. Joan poured tea and milk for them both, then read the letter.

Sue-Ellen could see that it was in her father's handwriting. She stood quietly behind her mother's shoulder and read:

Dear Joan

You and I have always loved fresh flowers, but they have to die. The dried flowers are beautiful too and they hold the memory of what we had. As long as the memory remains, so will our love.

Your own

Dudley

Joan understood that Dudley had planned the gift before he died. His first heart attack had taken place six months before the one that killed him. He knew another one was likely. That gave him time to plan a tribute to the passionate love he had shared with Joan for twenty-five years.

Sue-Ellen was sure it meant her dad was still alive some-where. She didn't talk about it to anyone; she didn't give away his game, but she resolved to wait for him. And wait she did.

She waited forty years before she finally admitted her father was dead. It was the strange result of a childhood dominated by secrecy, and by the mysterious disappearances and reappearances of her parents.

After the funeral, Joan collapsed. She went to bed and didn't stop crying for six months. For twenty-one years, she had been a perfect ASIO wife. She had protected her children and controlled their words and actions; she had joined the P&C and pumped the wives for information at meetings while Dudley charmed the husbands; she had baked every weekend for the family and the neighbourhood. She had held her nerve in a car chase with her family and the Petrovs inside. She was worryingly thin but, apart from that one terrible breakdown after her father's death, she was always in control. She was Dudley's able deputy twenty-four hours a day. When Dudley died, all that ended. She couldn't cope anymore.

Sue-Ellen remembers the six months after Dudley's death as a period of thick fog that they moved through slowly and drearily. Much of the detail of the time is lost in that fog, but certain events loom out of it: the funeral, a bus trip to Sydney with Joan to visit ASIO headquarters, legal proceedings that seemed to make no sense, a dismal Christmas party.

Until then, Sue-Ellen had been angry with Joan at times, but she had relied on her absolutely. Joan had told her what to do, what to say, what to wear and how to think. She had cooked her meals and fixed her hair. Suddenly, Sue-Ellen's mum was a weeping, raging child, angry with Dudley for leaving her and unable to imagine any way of living without him.

Sue-Ellen remembers looking around their house one day. Joan was crying; the house was a mess; there was nothing to eat. The faithful Shun Wahs had continued bringing food to their home for several weeks. Their kindness was inexhaustible, but Joan had eventually asked them to stop coming. She was embarrassed to still need their help but she had lost the energy to prepare meals and keep the household running.

Sue-Ellen had left school at fifteen to work at the Mutual Acceptance Company, a job she enjoyed, but now she quit her job and stayed home to help Joan. Instead of being a carefree girl with work and boyfriends and concerts, she was a companion, day and night, to Joan and Amanda. Mark had moved out of home by then.

One day Joan had a call from their bank manager. Their money was in the hands of the Public Curator Office, which was sorting out probate. 'Come and get some money out straightaway,' the bank manager advised Joan. 'The Public Curator says I have to freeze the account, but I'll wait till you've come down.' Sue-Ellen went with Joan to the bank to take out some money, and that kept them going—frugally—for six months.

There was one last contact from ASIO. They asked Joan to come to Sydney for a final debriefing. She and Sue-Ellen packed a small bag each and went to the grimy old bus depot at South Brisbane to catch a Greyhound bus. Grandma Doris arranged for them to stay with her sister-in-law, Mary, in Glebe. They sat silently for most of the eighteen-hour ride, staring out of the window as afternoon shadows deepened into night, sleeping in snatches, catching themselves dribbling on each other's shoulders or waking up with a quick snore. There was another bus trip when they arrived to take them to Aunt Mary, who was scary and made Sue-Ellen clean the bath as soon as she got out of it. More silence over cornflakes and hot tea and finally another bus to Agincourt. The fine four-storey building on the harbour at Potts Point was familiar to Joan but deeply impressive to Sue-Ellen, a place of fable, far away down south in the Big Smoke.

They were expected, and had no difficulty entering the building where they were ushered to the director-general's office. Joan's old friend Charles Spry had resigned in January 1970, but she was courteously received by his successor Peter Barbour. He wanted to talk to Joan on her own, so he summoned a young ASIO officer to take Sue-Ellen out for a drive.

Sue-Ellen remembers the director-general giving the young ASIO officer a long hard look. An expert at interpreting expressions, she knew what it meant: *You touch that girl and you die.* The young man behaved beautifully. He drove Sue-Ellen out to the Heads, which pleased her as she had never been there. They sat there and looked at the ocean. After a while, he bought her something to eat and then drove her back to rejoin her mother at Agincourt.

Joan's conversation with the director-general remains confidential, but the children observed that it confirmed and hardened Joan's determination to cut all ties with informants and to insist on the rule of silence. There was to be no discussion at all about their father's career and no contact with any of their old friends and acquaintances. The children were never certain whether it was okay still to talk to people like the Duddies or June Barton or old school friends—there was no way of knowing who might be an ASIO connection, and questions were forbidden. So they let those connections drop off, too. After that trip they were cut off entirely from their old life, except that a Canadian couple they had met in the old days arrived for an Australian holiday and came for Christmas dinner with the Dohertys. Much later in their lives, 'Uncle Mick' made a surprise appearance, but that was long after they had given up hope of seeing any of their old friends.

Joan cooked that Christmas meal but it was a miserable day of protracted polite conversation, punctuated by tears in the kitchen. Mark surprised them all by spending a ridiculous sum of money on Christmas presents. He gave Sue-Ellen a large bottle of Estée Lauder Youth Dew perfume, which was considered the ultimate luxury gift at the time. Sue-Ellen had never had such an expensive gift in her life. They couldn't speak about anything real, but Mark showed his love with gifts.

Mark wasn't around a lot, but he managed the legal proceedings with the Public Curator Office, which seemed endless and confusing. They were still continuing when Sue-Ellen realised they had run out of money. It had taken that long for them both to realise that no one was coming to rescue them.

She plucked up the courage to tell Joan one day while they were walking through Kmart. Joan gave Sue-Ellen one of her old, keen looks and said, 'You'd better go back to work. I'll have to get myself back together.' As soon as she said that, it seemed as if Joan's powers returned. She found a job in the hardware department at Myer and began making a new life for herself and for her family.

⌣

The fog lifted for Sue-Ellen too. She took a job as the PR rep for Kay's Rent-a-Car in the city, next to Festival Hall. She liked the job and she was having fun again. The wrestlers who put on nightly shows at Festival Hall became her friends and looked out for her. She joined Mark doing amateur theatre at La Boite. They threw themselves into acting and Sue-Ellen came home late after rehearsals and pot-smoking parties with friends. She and Mark both felt the theatre people were their real family at that time, and their refuge.

Joan sold the house at The Gap and moved the family to an apartment in Red Hill, closer to the city. She seemed to be fine, but she had changed. She was a good-looking woman and she started wearing the long skirts and boots that were in fashion in the seventies. She took up smoking and drinking. Sue-Ellen and Mark would come home to find their mother rolling joints with friends, while Amanda stayed in her bedroom. Joan seemed to have many new friends, mostly men. She was making up her own rules and having some fun after a lifetime of iron discipline and staying up late to wait for Dudley.

She had discovered that the sexual revolution applied to women too and she gloried in it. Instead of instructing Sue-Ellen to hang on to her virginity, Joan now urged her to lose it.

One awful night, Sue-Ellen had a visit from a boy she had once gone out with and still liked. He stayed on after she went to bed. Unusually restless, she woke in the night and heard noises from her mother's bedroom. Her old boyfriend had not gone home. He was with Joan and they were not sleeping.

The girls didn't recognise their mother at the time—and they were furious with her. Amanda, at thirteen, had a cutting tongue and she fought savagely with Joan. In the end, they stopped talking to each other entirely and just passed each other acid messages via Sue-Ellen.

Sue-Ellen decided that life at home was impossible. She thought that, if she left, Amanda and Joan would have to talk to each other. It was at this point that her hairdresser gave her the name of his friends in Sydney and suggested a holiday. Sue-Ellen acted quickly, packed her bag and left home. In Sydney, she found the love and closeness she had been missing, as well as the fun and fashion. And then she found Hugh.

Mark married young, too. Both he and Sue-Ellen were married by the time they were twenty-one. That left just Amanda at home, living alone with a woman she didn't recognise who was running amok like the teenager she had never had the chance to be. Amanda believed that her mother had stopped caring about her.

'Mum felt entitled to her life and she didn't want a dependent daughter anymore,' Amanda told Sue-Ellen and Mark. 'I wanted to study but she wanted me to go out to work as soon as possible. She kept arranging job interviews for me, some of them with her boyfriends, and she wouldn't rest until I got an apprenticeship as a hairdresser.'

When Amanda hit puberty, Joan presented her with a book called *And When She Was Bad She Was Popular*. It was a sex education manual, seventies style, a fictional story about a girl losing her virginity at seventeen.

'There was a subliminal message: you need to get laid and you'll be okay,' said Amanda. The young girl, whose only comfort was the church group she attended, was humiliated by the gift.

Amanda was lonely and desperately unhappy. One day, rummaging through her mother's bedroom drawer, she found a referral to a psychiatrist. The referral was for her, Amanda. Had her mother asked her GP to make out this referral for her? Did her mother think she was crazy? *Was* she crazy? Sometimes she felt like it, in this new world that made no sense.

She waited to see when her mother would raise the topic with her. How would she introduce the idea of visiting a psychiatrist? What would the psychiatrist be like? Maybe he would be kind. Maybe he could help her with this desperate grief she was feeling for her father and for the home she had grown up in and for the old life that had vanished.

Her mother never raised the topic and never took her to the psychiatrist. Amanda thought deeply about it for many years. She decided later that the doctor had thought she needed help but that her mother had chosen not to help her. She decided that her mother didn't *want* to help her.

She had no one to talk to. She had been close to Mark and Sue-Ellen but they had gone. When she did see them and tried to tell them what it was like at home, she felt that they didn't listen. She never felt they really heard her and believed her until they sat on Sue-Ellen's verandah together more than forty years later.

Six years after Dudley's death, Joan moved into a house with an old family friend called Roy, and Roy's teenage son. There was a room there for Amanda but she refused to go. She still desperately missed her father and she could not believe her mother would form a new relationship with a man Amanda thought was stupid and ordinary. She had a good job as a hairdresser, so she rented a flat and left to begin life alone. Joan married Roy four years later and stayed with him until his death.

The little family of spies, once so close and loving, had been shattered. Each of them lived their lives quite separately for many years. They kept in touch, they had annual family parties, but there was no real communication between them until ASIO knocked on the door again and set Sue-Ellen off on her quest to find the truth about her childhood.

⌒

All three Doherty children had been trained to mentally file away knowledge that was incompatible with the roles they played. If they were lunching with the Serbian Titches, it was dangerous to remember they had dined with the Croatian Titches the week before. If they saw their father taking photos of suspects, it was safest not to remember who those people were. Forgetting the facts of their lives was part of the complex adaptive strategy required for the children to stay safe while knowing about the family business. Both the girls, without having discussed it, had chosen to put their memories into a mental box and lock them away. Mark was able, more simply, to just put his head into a book and forget anything outside it. When they finally began to talk, he kept saying 'I don't remember anything about that', then would be surprised when he found that he did.

When their father died and Joan told them they were legally bound to never speak about ASIO business again, they knew what to do. They forgot about it in the ways they had practised all their lives. Except that this time it meant forgetting everything they had done as a family. ASIO work *was* their family life—there had been no time for anything else. It meant even forgetting their father. From then on, they had nothing real to speak to each other about. They needed urgently to create new lives for themselves, far removed from the ones they had shared. Mark and Sue-Ellen buried themselves in theatre and married young; Joan discovered the fun she'd missed out on all her life. Only Amanda, still a child, was unable to instantly create a new life. She had to live a life she passionately disliked, in her mother's wake, and she grieved alone for her father and the childhood she had lost.

During the years they had been apart, their childhood had become fainter and more dreamlike for all of them. For daily purposes, it was forgotten. When Sue-Ellen brought them together to discuss the past, when it was no longer forbidden to talk, their first task was to bring those memories back into their conscious minds. They needed to decide what was real and what was dreamed or imagined. Each time they found they had remembered the same thing was a small victory. Each face, each name, each place, each story brought another piece of their hidden life into the open.

Forgetting their childhoods had been essential for their survival, but it came at a cost. They lost their sense of who they really were and of what they valued. They lost the sense of belonging that they had taken for granted as children, of being part of a close family. They lost their place in the world. Each fact they verified by talking to each other reduced the fear of the unknown and eased their sense of aloneness. Each fact helped to knit their family back into existence.

18

The Deceptions of Memory

Sue-Ellen, Mark and Amanda verified many facts quite easily just by talking to each other. If they all remembered the same thing, with the same names and dates, they called it a fact. They checked some less certain memories with Joan or by searching through photos or family documents. They were programmed to forget, but they had also been trained to remember facts precisely, so their powers of accurate recall were probably greater than those of the average person.

Sometimes one of them had a vivid and detailed memory that the others could not confirm. For example, Sue-Ellen clearly remembered the unnamed ASIO agents taking her father's wooden leg on the day after he had died. For her, the wooden leg had been as much a part of her father as his other leg and the thought of this brutal theft had horrified her for forty years. Joan told her that she had buried the leg with Dudley, but Sue-Ellen's memory was so clear and explicit that she didn't believe her mother. She asked Amanda and Mark about it several times until, finally, something about their polite embarrassment got through to her. She recognised that, vivid as it seemed, this was a false memory.

In this way, they discovered that our memories are not objective facts. All of us notice certain things and not others. And we change our memories as we take them out and look at them; we change a sequence of events or a length of time. Everyone has had the experience of thinking an incident only lasted five minutes and discovering later that it had taken an hour. And, especially when strong emotions are involved, we can file false information—based on assumptions or misperceptions—into the filing cabinet we call memory. The ASIO agents had intruded at a time of great loss and looted (as Sue-Ellen saw it) items that Sue-Ellen considered parts of Dudley's person—like the lock-picking kit, which she coveted, and the cameras. Her highly emotional state, the speed at which events took place, the fact that she was the only family member who hadn't been at home when her father died, and the fact that she couldn't speak about it afterwards all created a perfect set-up for a young girl to imagine and remember something that simply didn't happen.

The most disturbing false belief that Sue-Ellen hung onto, for decades after her father's death, was the idea that he was still alive somewhere. For anyone outside the family, it is hard to understand how that idea could have persisted so powerfully in an otherwise sane and highly observant adult. Sue-Ellen found it hard to understand too. Once she started talking to people about it, she concluded wryly that the idea was largely the result of high levels of unfiltered childhood exposure to news and current affairs.

One summer day, when Sue-Ellen was fourteen, Australian prime minister Harold Holt walked into Cheviot Beach in Victoria for a swim and never came out. The police said he had drowned, but his body was never found. Sue-Ellen followed the incident avidly in the media and wondered what had really happened to him.

Had she been able to ask her mother about it, she might have been told that Harold Holt was a stubborn man who had refused to listen to sound advice about not going into the water that day. That was Joan's opinion on the matter. But Sue-Ellen was not allowed to ask her parents questions about politics or espionage. As always, she had to work things out for herself.

Years later, a former naval officer alleged that the prime minister had been picked up by a Chinese submarine and had been spying for the Chinese for thirty years. Sue-Ellen followed the Titcombe allegations with fascination, but still didn't feel confident to discuss these or any public events with other people. She also read in great detail about the shocking defections of British spies Burgess, Maclean and Philby. If that could happen, she reasoned, why couldn't an Australian prime minister be a Chinese spy?

What Sue-Ellen had worked out in her solitary research was that when people disappear mysteriously and people think they are dead, it ain't necessarily so.

In the case of her father, that belief made perfect sense. He was always disappearing mysteriously to do important work, and he always came back. As a child, she saw him as a superhero keeping the world safe. Most children have those sorts of ideas, but they gradually learn that their parents are not gods, just flawed human beings, through the inevitable disappointments of growing up. Sue-Ellen never got that reality check because of the inability to ask questions before his early death and the oath of silence that bound them afterwards.

When Dudley died, all the rich, varied and sometimes dazzling people in their lives disappeared too. All the ASIO uncles, the Chinese informants, the African-American sailors, the geisha girl and the motorbike policemen—all the people Dudley had charmed into their lives—were gone. They were at the house after he died; they were there at the funeral; and then, as suddenly as if they had all died too, they were not there anymore.

The world of her childhood had vanished. So Sue-Ellen did the only thing she could do: she forgot about it. She found out what other people thought was the normal way to live and she learned to live like that. She did a good job of it.

Until the day Joan confirmed that Dudley had really died, and Sue-Ellen finally believed her, a deep part of her—so secret that even she didn't know about it most of the time—had been waiting for her father to return from whatever mission he was on. For decades the child spy had lived in deep cover inside the woman, waiting to be reactivated.

19

The Fix-It Man

One of the things Sue-Ellen most wanted to clear up was the question of her father's character. By this time, she recognised that she had idolised her father and that no one could be the magnificent flying immortal she had imagined him to be. She still loved him but she needed to be sure that he was not a bad man. She had grown up thinking of the world in black and white ways: communism versus the free world, good versus evil, heroes versus villains. Unlike Mark and Amanda, she wasn't an extensive reader, so had not learned about the subtleties of character through storytelling. She couldn't help fearing that if her father was not a hero, he must be a villain.

Between them, Mark and Amanda examined their father's habits, his lies, his talents and his qualities to see if they could help Sue-Ellen reach the understanding she needed. The main difficulty they faced was that work and home were so intertwined for the Dohertys that it was impossible to know where one started and the other finished. Given that concealing things was part of his job, and everything he did was work, it was hard to extract Dudley the person from the ASIO man.

'Pick someone famous who reminds you of Dad,' challenged Sue-Ellen.

Mark and Amanda looked uncertain.

'I think: Bill Clinton,' said Sue-Ellen.

After a short silence, they all laughed.

'Okay,' said Mark. 'Because he had a kind of cheeky boyishness and, at the same time, an aura of being solid, dependable, someone you could trust.'

'A lot of people thought he was a cop,' said Amanda. 'He was good at being non-specific when he befriended people.'

'He'd ask leading questions without giving away any information about himself,' said Mark.

'Brisbane is, and always was, a Catholic community, and Dad was quite happy for people to believe he was Catholic if it was going to help him to get to know someone better,' Amanda observed.

'It was assumed,' Mark added. 'Because back in those days it was the "Micks" and the Protestants, Masons and non-Masons, secret handshakes and signs and all that.'

They debated about whether Dudley had really believed in UFOs. Sue-Ellen thought he had; Mark thought it was just about getting to know 'people of interest'.

They wondered whether Dudley had changed his political beliefs near the end of his life. He had marched in an anti-Vietnam demonstration. He might have been working undercover but Mark had overheard a conversation between his parents that revealed he had got into a lot of trouble for marching. Mark hoped that his father, the rusted-on Liberal, had come out against that war, but they would never know.

Amanda remembered asking her father how he made decisions. He told her: 'There's good and there's bad and there's something in between. There's right and there's wrong and there's something that can hurt people.'

Amanda looked at her brother and sister. 'As a child I didn't understand, but later on I realised he was right. There's always a grey area. And Dad lived in the grey area.'

They questioned everything about him, even his unstinting generosity. All those gifts and meals, the time he spent helping Chinese people bring family members to Australia. Was it real, or was it for work? They weren't sure what they thought until, during one session, Hugh chimed in with a comment. He had joined them quietly on the verandah to sit in the background and listen. At the talk of Dudley's generosity, he snorted. 'Come on! That was the currency he used for getting information from people.'

That united the Dohertys instantly. 'No!' They all spoke at once.

'Mum and Dad felt we were well off and other people, particularly migrants and people who had a tough background, needed a bit of help,' said Mark.

'They did a lot for people that didn't get them anything in return,' said Sue-Ellen.

'They really cared,' said Amanda.

They all saw themselves as cynical people and they were willing to question and examine the evidence on any topic.

But at the first sign of outside criticism, their response was unequivocal. They realised that, deep down, they believed that their parents, however flawed, were generous and good people.

When their dad died, Sue-Ellen had wondered who would fix things now. 'And I didn't mean mechanical things,' she clarified.

'The world,' said Amanda. It had been the same for her.

'He got me out of scrapes many a time, juggling things behind the scenes and setting things right,' said Mark. 'He was a good fix-it man.'

'That's who he was,' laughed Sue-Ellen. 'Dudley Doherty was a great fix-it man.'

20

The Price They Paid

The Doherty children had all followed the news stories about the Foley boys and liked to compare their situation with their own. Tim and Alex Foley had grown up in an average family, first in Canada, then moving over the border to Cambridge, Massachusetts, in the US. Their mum was a soccer mum and their dad worked in a consulting firm. Theirs was a close family, and they had plenty of friends.

When the Doherty kids were little, and they had to say their dad worked for the Attorney-General's Department, they had wished he had an interesting job like the fathers who were milkmen or who worked at the markets. So they could relate to the Foley boys, who thought their parents were boring compared with the parents of their friends.

The Foley parents ceased to be boring on Tim's twentieth birthday, on 27 June 2010. That was the night the FBI, armed with battering rams, burst through the door of their house. Tim thought he had been busted for underage drinking at his birthday party. When the agents handcuffed his parents and took them away in separate cars, he was sure they had made a mistake.

But the FBI had not made a mistake. Not only were the boys' parents Russian spies, they had actually been born in Russia. Their names were not Donald Heathfield and Tracey Foley but Andrei Bezrukov and Elena Vavilova—KGB-trained secret agents.

The family was deported to Russia. The two boys couldn't even pronounce their own names in Russian, and everything about their new home was strange and unfamiliar. A woman dropped by and they heard she was their grandmother but they couldn't talk to her—she didn't speak English and they didn't speak Russian. They didn't feel welcome in Moscow. Yet they had been stripped of their Canadian citizenship. They had lost their home, their friends, their career hopes and their easy trust in their parents. It was a devastating series of losses.

Six years later, the boys went public in an interview with Shaun Walker of *The Guardian*. They wanted to win back Canadian citizenship, and they hoped to gain public support for their long legal battle. Stories circulated that the boys had been groomed by their parents as spies, but the boys denied it vehemently. Why, after all, would their parents have taken the risk of telling their children their true identities? Tim and Alex said it was unfair they should be punished for the sins of their parents.

Alex told the journalist that he sometimes wondered why his parents decided to have children at all. He said he had wrestled with the question of whether he hated his parents and felt betrayed by them. In the end, he concluded that they were the same people who had raised him lovingly, whatever secrets they had hidden. Tim didn't say whether he had come to the same conclusion.

It took several years of protracted legal battles before both boys won back their Canadian citizenship, allowing them to live again in North America.

The Foleys had decided not to tell their children about their spying lives. This is the usual decision that spies make. It protects national secrets—what the kids don't know, they can't tell—and it allows children the chance to grow up as normal kids. Unless their parents' cover is blown, of course, which is what happened to Tim and Alex. That's the risk.

The Dohertys made an unconventional choice about raising their children. They weighed up the pros and cons of telling and not telling, and decided they would trust their children with the truth. Dudley and Joan had both come from toxic, secret-keeping families and they didn't want that for their children.

So how did it work out for the children when they grew up? Would they have been happier, less anxious, more 'normal' if they had grown up in blissful ignorance of the whole business of ASIO? It's impossible to know, but Sue-Ellen, Mark and Amanda wanted to work out what they had gained and what they had lost in their unusual upbringing. They talked with each other about how things had gone for them when they grew up. Much remains private for these extremely private people, but these things are on the record.

Amanda married George, a Greek Cypriot whom she met when she was working as an apprentice hairdresser. He was a kind man from a large family, and the package of George and the family felt like something big and permanent and substantial for Amanda to belong to. They fell in love and had a big fat Greek wedding and Amanda was instantly part of a family and a history and a culture. She desperately wanted to belong, but she was too independent to fit into the role of a young Greek bride. That marriage lasted a year.

Next she married a man from one of the two categories of men her father had forbidden the girls to ever marry: biker cops and Yugoslavians. When Amanda told her mother she was marrying a Yugoslavian man, Joan said, 'Your father would turn in his grave.' Once again, Amanda had married a man deeply grounded in a big family and a big history, something she longed for in theory but couldn't bear in practice. Her new father-in-law saw her as secondhand goods, and nothing secondhand was good enough for his son. Amanda couldn't fit into that family either but could not regret the marriage that produced her daughter, Nina.

Amanda raised Nina alone and they have a strong, close bond. Amanda is a quiet and forceful speaker. She sits very straight and makes witty remarks; she is articulate and formidable. But she bends her head if Nina speaks, and defers to her daughter's memory and judgement. Nina is the person she trusts.

Amanda is reserved. Nina was surprised when she found that children she knew lived in homes where people dropped in, or where guests were entertained frequently or casually. In her family home, entertaining was rare and carefully planned, and it was not uncommon for Amanda to be stricken by one of her fierce migraines just before the event took place. Amanda copes with difficulties alone, behind closed doors.

She never talks to anyone about politics. 'Knock yourselves out,' she says to her colleagues at work around election time. 'I'm not joining this conversation. I had more politics than any child should experience when I was growing up.' Politics was a taboo subject even at home—she has never told Nina what party she votes for. (It seems that repression doesn't work: Nina went on to study politics at university.)

At school, Mark Doherty was the all-round high achiever in science, maths, art, music and performance. He read constantly, did science experiments and saved up his pocket money for musical instruments. People mistook him for a conservative like his father because he was serious, courteous and scholarly. But like the rest of his family, he formed his own independent views. He loved rational argument but, as a kid, he was crazy about flying saucers; he invented his own language Venutian and taught himself to speak it. He read *MAD Magazine*, with its mix of impudent satire and social commentary. He turned down, on principle, the offer of going to an expensive private school (an offer Sue-Ellen and Amanda would have loved to have taken up, but they weren't given the chance because they weren't boys). At the state school he attended, he turned down the offer of being a prefect. He didn't want to be any kind of authority figure.

Dudley thought that Mark would grow out of his leftist beliefs, but he never did. He believes in equality and fairness, but he speaks about politics with an ironic tone and is never dogmatic. He chose a career in optometry; the child spy, trained to watch, grew up to take care of people's eyes.

Sue-Ellen and Amanda mythologise Mark a little—their brilliant older brother, the mad scientist, the solitary figure, the muso. He doesn't buy into their idea of him as an eccentric genius. He points to his failures. He dropped out of university the first time he tried, the year his father died. He spent eight years in the public service and other jobs he didn't like before going back to university to retrain.

He married young and has two beloved daughters, Sorelle and Cara, though that marriage didn't last. Sue-Ellen's daughter Phoebe once remarked that Mark was an island. She said he loved his girls and his music, and that was all. But he also visits his mother every week, taking her shopping, doing little errands and listening quietly to her news. He recently announced his engagement to Denise, and his sisters are happy for him.

Sue-Ellen's marriage lasted and continues to make her glad. She and Hugh raised their children together and cherish them. They have had financial ups and downs but, overall, they are well off. But Sue-Ellen is aware that she achieved all that by splitting herself into two people for most of her life, up until she could talk freely with Amanda and Mark. Throughout her career, Sue-Ellen knocked back several offers of work that might have been lucrative: jobs as a television actress or a model. Mostly unconsciously, her childhood training in invisibility held her back. She couldn't go public, even though she longed to. She had a brief period of freedom in Sydney, being as flamboyant as she wanted, but that was only possible because she was fitting in with a group of people who all behaved like that and it was never a long-term proposition.

There is a sense about all three of the Doherty siblings of something held back, held in, restrained. Of exceptional people who have chosen to stay in the shadows.

They are intensely private, each in different ways. Sue-Ellen is loud and talkative with a warm manner, but it took her many years to be able to express her real opinion about anything. A lot of her talk disguises the fact that she is watching, noticing, assessing the person she is talking to and everyone else in the room.

They are still watchers. They know exactly what cars are parked on their street at any time and whether any of those cars are out of place. They remember numberplates automatically. They also remember faces, dates, names. They silently notice when people say things that conflict with other things they have said or with other aspects of their appearance or lifestyle.

Self-expression is more difficult for them than for most people in our culture. Historian Ray Evans grew up in Queensland in the same era as the Dohertys and he remembers the old Labour Day marches the Dohertys attended as being desultory and depressing, with men dressed in dark suits, wearing badges. 'It wasn't a flamboyant time,' Evans told me. 'All passions were underground. On the surface it was dull and conformist. The communists were brave but even they were boring and rigid and buttoned down. Young people wanted to be free.'

Evans and other teenagers in the sixties seized their freedom: they wore bright clothes, grew their hair long, bought banned books and listened to rock 'n' roll. Until Dudley died in 1970, the Dohertys had to watch other people enjoying their freedom while strictly conforming themselves. Mark protested quietly by reading *MAD Magazine* and listening to imported records of blues music, but he never jeopardised his father's work by breaking out publicly. At a time when self-expression was the new way to be, the Doherty kids had to stay buttoned down.

Only Joan broke out into wildness, after Dudley's death. The children were perhaps too well trained by fear to ever fully lose their sense of restraint.

There is one way they have long expressed themselves exuberantly: by dressing up in carefully controlled situations. Every year, more than once, they arrange a huge costume party with a theme. It might be Mexican or a Harry Potter theme, or they wear balloon hats or moustaches or funny spectacles, or go country or bling. They have costume parties at Christmas and twenty-first parties, and Sue-Ellen's daughter Phoebe swears her wedding will be a theme wedding. They go all out. They make their own costumes, decorate their houses and cook special food, and research the theme or historical period so they can keep up the conversation in character all night. These events brought them together before they were able to talk to each other about their lives, and they continue today.

They set clear rules for each event and follow them to the letter. As Sue-Ellen says firmly, 'You can't half-arse it. You have to do it properly.'

As children they had to commit fully to each role they were asked to play. Dudley would brief them on how to behave, and what they could and couldn't say and do, and they would follow his directions carefully. That was scary for small children, having language, behaviour and clothes all strictly controlled, and not being able to make any mistakes. As adults, they choose to play roles, but now they make the rules themselves. They have permission to be expressive and have fun. By putting on a fake moustache or a funny hat, and doing it wholeheartedly, they can be fully expressive beings. All three of them love it.

Self-expression in other forms still feels risky. Amanda and Mark think of Sue-Ellen as the family extrovert. So they were startled when she confessed that she had seen someone she knew in a shop the day before and had ducked behind the freezer so the woman couldn't see her.

'She was a perfectly nice person, just a neighbour,' Sue-Ellen explained. 'I have a strong urge to avoid people in a wide-open environment. I always duck, or cross the road, or pretend not to see people.' Behind her appearance of confidence lies a little girl who is still terrified of saying the wrong thing and acutely aware that any encounter, however slight, might lead to betrayal, disgrace or the disappearance of someone she loves. Her ducking and hiding turned into automatic behaviour that she didn't even notice herself. Sue-Ellen hid her fears behind a façade of extroversion; she learned how to hide in full view. When she finally talked about it to Amanda and Mark, she felt that she was waking from a long sleep, looking around with surprise at her world and at herself.

Sue-Ellen has only ever seen Mark cry twice. The first time was on the night their father died. After Mark had made all the phone calls and sorted out all the people, he went out to the verandah of their house. Sue-Ellen found him there, sobbing his heart out. The second time was on Sue-Ellen's verandah forty years later. It happened when they were talking about trust.

During the time I worked with Sue-Ellen on this book, she spoke to me several times about how difficult it was for her to trust people. It seemed that she always looked for reasons not to trust people, where other people might look for reasons *to* trust. She had difficulty trusting her parents, and it had taken Hugh years to win her trust. She mentioned to Mark and Amanda that the inability to trust was one of the casualties of spying. The children were taught very early that they could not trust anyone.

They discussed the topic playfully, as usual, discussing the people they knew and why they trusted some—just a few—but not others. They discovered, with surprise, that they trusted people who were open.

'That's weird, isn't it?' asked Nina, who was part of the audience on the verandah that day.

'Yep, because we're so closed,' agreed Sue-Ellen.

'Show me your hand and I'll think about showing you mine,' laughed Amanda.

Mark was silent. His sisters waited for him to speak.

'I was thinking about Mike,' he said at last. Mike was a member of a band that Mark played with.

'You don't trust him?' asked Sue-Ellen.

'No. No. It's the opposite. I *do* trust him. He's a member of a Christian fundamentalist church, which is something I strongly disagree with. And yet. Oh excuse me.' He was crying now. 'And yet he's somebody I'd trust my life with.'

Sue-Ellen and Amanda were crying with him then. They sat together, deeply united, recognising the great difficulty they all had in trusting people and celebrating that the impossible had happened—that Mark felt completely safe and open with someone he would have disapproved of on paper, and that this experience was so rare and lovely, it had reduced him to tears.

21

Still Working

If Dudley was Bill Clinton, then perhaps Joan was Hilary. Always there, always working, routinely betrayed by her husband, lacking his easy charm. She was the hard taskmaster, the rule enforcer, as the children grew up. Dudley delivered the beatings, but it was always Joan's decision. The children laughed at her snobbery and feared her cold, fair judgement. After Dudley's death, when she took on a new persona and reversed all her strict rules, the children were shocked. Sue-Ellen felt that nothing made sense and wondered if her mother was a hypocrite. Amanda was sure her mother didn't care about her and wanted to be rid of her. Mark didn't say what he thought; he never ceased in his gentle care for his mother, but he distanced himself and came to the family as a visitor.

On the verandah, Amanda saw that Mark and Sue-Ellen listened to her with love and attention. In the relief of finally speaking and being believed, she started to question her old interpretation of why her mother had hidden the referral to the psychiatrist.

'I thought Mum didn't want to help me, but maybe she just didn't want to tell a psychiatrist about our family. Maybe she was scared of letting out the secrets.'

Sue-Ellen and Mark nodded thoughtfully. It made sense and they were glad that Amanda could feel a slight relief from her sense of being abandoned at that time.

Later they talked about the things Joan had taught them: the skills of observation, the appreciation of different kinds of people, the ability to notice without judging. They were fair-minded people and they realised Joan had done her best for them.

While they were speaking about her, Joan was living in a retirement village overlooked by the turrets and car parks of the Westfield Carindale shopping complex. Her hair was white. She had a tumour on her spine and scoliosis, so she lived in constant pain. Words that used to come so easily were not always easy to retrieve. She was alone now that both of her husbands had died.

As she sat at her kitchen table one morning, she heard a knock at the door and a friendly bearded face appeared around it.

'G'day, Jo,' said the man.

'Come on in, Norm,' she answered. 'There's a drink for you in the fridge.'

Norm worked at the retirement village and he looked after all the residents as well as he could, but he did a few special things for his mate Jo. He walked in and helped himself to a soft drink from the fridge. He knew where the glasses were.

'Hey Jo, you've been wondering when the new people are moving into number six?' he asked.

'That's right, Norm. Weren't they supposed to come yesterday?'

'Yep. But they're not moving in till Monday now. Bet you can't guess what I found outside their front window.'

'What was that, Norm?'

'I found your walking stick,' he grinned. 'Just checking them out, were you?'

'Oh, is that where I left it?' said Joan, smiling at him. 'I couldn't find it.'

Joan had always watched her neighbours carefully, ready to notice the odd things that didn't fit, like the wrong pieces in a puzzle. Occasionally, rarely, she would decide something was worth reporting to ASIO. By the time she reached her eighties she was still keeping an eye out, although she no longer made any reports. She saw a lot of people in the retirement village going in and out of each other's units and talking, but she tried to get to know the ones who sat very quietly, because she realised they knew more about what was going on.

Sue-Ellen was angry at the way ASIO had treated her mother, at the way they had cut her loose like a piece of old string when Dudley died. But Joan had never lost the faith. She knew that ASIO was necessary for the safety of Australia. And she missed the work. Missed it every day. The country girl who had wanted to be a doctor, who dreamed of getting an education, still loved the chance to use her brain and solve puzzles. The little girl who had no control over the attacks by her father had protected her sister and herself as much as possible by watching and listening. Later she used those skills to protect her family and her country: watching, noticing, keeping secrets, fighting evil.

Before going off to do his other chores, Norm chaffed her kindly for a few minutes. Occasionally Joan asked him a question about what was going on in the retirement village.

'No use asking me, Jo. You know all the news first,' he said, rinsing his glass at the sink.

If ASIO ever comes back to recruit Joan, she will be ready. She has never stopped working for them.

Epilogue

2020

Nine years have passed since the ASIO men and Dr Rhys Crawley came to interview Joan for their history, setting Sue-Ellen free to talk about the past with her brother and sister. In Canberra, ASIO has built a grand edifice on a site the size of three city blocks to house its rapidly growing staff. These staff, hired increasingly for their high-level technical skills, can gaze out the window at Lake Burley Griffin or at Parliament House. It is a different world from the Cold War ASIO, which had its dingy, secret buildings and its suspicion of computers. ASIO wields great power in the land and everyone knows it. Sue-Ellen can't believe that you can look it up on a website; no one pretends that spies don't exist anymore. Like the Dohertys, ASIO has come out of hiding.

For months now, Mark, Sue-Ellen and Amanda have been collaborating on a special project. They have been making a wedding gift for Mark's daughter Cara: a multicoloured crocheted rug. Today they have come to Sue-Ellen's house to admire it, draped over the long wooden dining table. Instead of being made in squares, each patch is in the shape of a flower. Every member of the family, including all the children and grandchildren, have crocheted the flowers and have met to sew them together. It is a work of art and a work of love. Nothing half-arsed about it, as Sue-Ellen would say.

After their momentous conversation on the verandah, the siblings have continued to see each other regularly. They don't need to talk about the past anymore and there is no need for reserve with each other, now that they have pieced their stories together into a colourful whole. They have stitched themselves into a family again.

Amanda's daughter, Nina, and Sue-Ellen's daughter, Phoebe, are there to admire the rug and Nina has some news.

'They've asked me at uni if I want to apply for work with ASIO,' she says. 'It's what they think I'm good for.'

Nobody at university knows Nina's family background but her teachers say she has the right skills for the work: good listening skills, an analytical mind, powers of observation and 'context-specific information', strategic thinking, problem solving, and writing.

'What did you tell them?' asked Sue-Ellen.

'No, of course. They've asked me before and I always say no.'

Nina intends to marry one day and she wants a full family unit, with both parents around. So, *anything* but an ASIO career.

Phoebe laughs. She has taken up the other great family interest (other than spying, that is) in design and costume. She has become an interior designer and already has an international reputation.

'I can't believe ASIO hasn't asked *me* to join,' she says.

'They don't need their interior refit done,' says Amanda.

'They'd be like, "What did you do last Thursday?" Um, I don't know,' says Phoebe.

They all laugh—the two mothers relieved and secretly amazed that their children can be the people they want to be.

Acknowledgements

My first thanks go to the Doherty family: Joan, Mark, Sue-Ellen and Amanda. It took courage to speak to me after a lifetime of silence. They did it with good humour and impeccable manners. I am grateful that they trusted me; I know now that trust is the hardest thing of all for people trained in spy craft.

Three friends stayed with me for the course of this book. Bev Sullivan started the whole thing by recommending me when Sue-Ellen was looking for a journalist. She provided moral and literary support throughout the process, including a thrilling demonstration of how to create a book structure by shuffling cards on her pool table.

Kristina Olsson gave up precious time from her own writing life to closely read two drafts of *With My Little Eye* and to give exacting feedback, which somehow made me want to write another draft. She listened to me talking about this book as we walked through many miles of rainforest. I don't know how she felt after those walks, but I always felt hopeful and glad.

Jenny Gilmore was my email writing buddy: she is a social worker and is writing a must-read book about how to heal childhood trauma. We thought at first that our writing projects were totally different but we could motivate each other to meet deadlines. As it turned out, Jenny's book helped me understand a lot about the Doherty family and her comments on my writing were perceptive and helpful.

These people helped me with reading the manuscript at various stages; lending me writing spaces with views; or other practical assistance: Charlotte Wood, Carolyn Swindell, Nike Sulway, Dan Troy, Elvyne Hogan, Dell Smout, Tanya Milne-Jones, Bev Fitzgerald and Kate Ellis.

I always wanted Allen & Unwin to publish *With My Little Eye*, because of its outstanding collection of Australian spy histories. I believed this story could add a personal note to those eminent histories, showing what it was like for ASIO family members. What I didn't know was what a delightful experience it would be to work with publishing professionals like the ones at A&U. Commissioning publisher Elizabeth Weiss has been a kindly, astute presence throughout the process. I have always felt like she has my interests at heart. I am very grateful to Samantha Kent and Emma Driver for their meticulous, intelligent and helpful editing. Thanks also to Samantha Mansell for making administrative matters easy.

Love and thanks to Rosa, Annette, Peadar, Lynette, Isabella, Carrick, Susie Q, Patrick, Archie, Dan and Maria. Also to Jennifer and our Wednesday night yoga-and-talking-about-books-and-the-universe group. To Susan Johnson for her long and generous support for my writing. And to Emma Felton, my encouraging friend.

And, most particularly to Danny. I am so lucky to have you in my life.

⌣

This book could not have been written unless David Horner had written *The Spy Catchers: The Official History of ASIO, 1949–1963*. This fascinating history, published in 2014, officially confirmed that the Dohertys had been ASIO agents. Because the history included the names of the Dohertys and a photo of them with the Petrovs, it released the family to speak for the first time about their careers in espionage. They would never have spoken to me otherwise. Professor Horner's principal research officer, Dr Rhys Crawley, was also kind enough to give me his impressions of the Doherty story and to confirm some dates.

I relied on *The Spy Catchers* and its sequel, *The Protest Years: The Official History of ASIO, 1963–1975* by John Blaxland, for the ASIO context for the Doherty story. My copies of these two much-read books are full of notes and exclamation marks and even, for reasons I can't remember, pressed flowers. As I explored a world of secrets and disguises, it was immensely reassuring to have two fat volumes of authorised facts close to my elbow, and I thought of them as friends.

Agent Sonya: Lover, Mother, Soldier, Spy (UK: Penguin Books, 2020) by British espionage writer Ben Macintyre is an exciting true-life spy story about a successful Soviet military intelligence officer who was known and liked as a housewife and scone-baker in the quiet English village where she lived with her family. Reading it, I was moved to discover that Agent Sonya had many of the same concerns as Joan Doherty and that her children, like the Doherty children, had lifelong difficulties with trust in relationships.

Other books I read that informed or intrigued me about the world that the Dohertys lived and worked in included:

Mark Aarons, *The Family File,* Melbourne: Black Inc, 2010.

Mark Colvin, *Light and Shadow: Memoirs of a Spy's Son,* Melbourne: Melbourne University Press, 2016.

John Fahey, *Traitors and Spies: Espionage and Corruption in High Places in Australia, 1901–50,* Sydney: Allen & Unwin, 2020.

Robert Manne, *The Petrov Affair: Politics and Espionage,* Sydney: Pergamon, 1987.

David McKnight, *Australia's Spies and Their Secrets,* Sydney: Allen & Unwin, 1994.

Vladimir Petrov & Evdokia Petrov, *Empire of Fear: The Petrovs, Their Own Story,* London: Andre Deutsch, 1956.

Tony Reeves, *Mr Sin: The Abe Saffron Dossier,* Sydney: Allen & Unwin, 2007.

Alan Saffron, *Gentle Satan: My Father, Abe Saffron,* Australia: Penguin Books, 2008.

Molly J. Sasson, *More Cloak Than Dagger: One Woman's Career in Secret Intelligence,* Ballarat, Vic.: Connor Court Publishing, 2015.

Nicholas Whitlam & John Stubbs, *Nest of Traitors: The Petrov Affair,* Brisbane: Jacaranda Press, 1974.

Peter Wright, *Spy Catcher: The Candid Autobiography of a Senior Intelligence Officer,* Melbourne: William Heinemann, 1987.

∽

ASIO files are mostly kept in the National Archives of Australia and it was a thrill to discover that historical treasure trove. Sue-Ellen and I both visited the National Archives to see their exhibition *Spy: Espionage in Australia* in 2019. It was a pleasure to walk around with Sue-Ellen as she identified pieces of equipment she remembered from her childhood and saw photos of those Holden cars and even the same tie her father used to wear.

Thanks also to librarians at the State Library of Queensland who helped me with pressing questions of local history like 'Where was the brothel on Coronation Drive in the 1960s?'. Librarians are my favourite people.

∽

The scorpion medallion shown on the cover is an 'ASIO Retired Officers' Medallion' and is awarded to officers who retire after ten years' service. It was presented to the Doherty family in December 1996 in recognition of the service Dudley provided between 1949 and 1970 to ASIO and ultimately, through it, to the people of Australia. Sue-Ellen believes that her father was among the first to receive one.